Unquiet Americans

Other Books of Interest from St. Augustine's Press

Gerard V. Bradley, *Essays on Law, Religion, and Morality*

Christopher Kaczor (editor), *O Rare Ralph McInerny:*
Stories and Reflection on a Legendary Notre Dame Professor

Christopher Kaczor, *The Gospel of Happiness:*
How Secular Psychology Points to the Wisdom of Christian Practice

Kenneth D. Whitehead (editor), *The Church, Marriage, & the Family*

Alain Besançon, *Protestant Nation*

James V. Schall, *At a Breezy Time of Day:*
Selected Schall Interviews on Just about Everything

James V. Schall, *The Praise of 'Sons of Bitches':*
On the Worship of God by Fallen Men

James V. Schall, *The Regensburg Lecture*

Gary M. Bouchard, *Southwell's Sphere: The Influence of England's Secret Poet*

Charles R. Embry and Glenn Hughes (editors), *Timelessness of Proust:*
Reflections on In Search of Lost Time

Frederic Raphael and Joseph Epstein, *Where Were We?*

Étienne Gilson, *Theology and the Cartesian Doctrine of Freedom*

Josef Kleutgen, S.J., *Pre-Modern Philosophy Defended*

Charles Cardinal Journet, *The Mass: The Presence of the Sacrifice of the Cross*

Edward Feser, *The Last Superstition: A Refutation of the New Atheism*

Ernest A. Fortin, A.A., *Christianity and Philosophical Culture in the Fifth*
Century: The Controversy about the Human Soul in the West

Peter Kreeft, *Ecumenical Jihad*

Peter Kreeft, *Socrates' Children: The 100 Greatest Philosophers*

Josef Pieper, *The Christian Idea of Man*

Josef Pieper and Heinz Raskop, *What Catholics Believe*

Karl Rahner, *Encounters with Silence*

Roger Scruton, *An Intelligent Person's Guide to Modern Culture*

Unquiet Americans

U.S. Catholics, Moral Truth, and the Preservation of Civil Liberties

Gerard V. Bradley

St. Augustine's Press
South Bend, Indiana

Copyright @ 2019 by Gerard V. Bradley

All rights reserved. No part of this book may be reproduced, stored in a retrieval system, or transmitted, in any form or by any means, electronic, mechanical, photocopying, recording, or otherwise, without the prior permission of St. Augustine's Press.

Manufactured in the United States of America.

1 2 3 4 5 6   25 24 23 22 21 20 19

Library of Congress Cataloging in Publication Data
Bradley, Gerard V., 1954–
Unquiet Americans: U.S. Catholics and America's common good / Gerard V. Bradley. – 1st [edition].
        pages cm
ISBN 978-1-58731-104-8 (paperbound: alk. paper)
1. Common good – Religious aspects – Catholic Church. 2. Christianity and politics – Catholic Church. 3. Christianity and politics – United States. 4. Catholic Church – United States. I. Title.
BX1793.B73 2013
282'.73 – dc23   2013027533

∞ The paper used in this publication meets the minimum requirements of the American National Standard for Information Sciences - Permanence of Paper for Printed Materials, ANSI Z39.48-1984.

St. Augustine's Press
www.staugustine.net

Contents

Introduction

The United States is a "nation conceived in liberty" and freedom has been at the core of Americans' self-understanding ever since. This "liberty" always included a collective component – the right of the people to govern themselves politically; what we call *democracy*. But the term "self-government" was long ago drafted in support of the more central notion of "liberty": each adult *person's* independence from the arbitrary authority of another, the right to direct one's own life towards genuine human fulfillment by and through free choices and, in that specific way, to be the author of one's own life. This meaning of "liberty" in large measure defined our nation. Denials of this right to persons who deserved to enjoy it have not been rare in American history. The enslavement of African-Americans and the enforced servility of women, for example, were not only immoral. These practices also betrayed our political ideals. They were un-American.

When the United States Supreme Court declared on June 29, 1992, that "[a]t the heart of liberty is the right to define one's own concept of existence, of meaning, of the universe, and of the mystery of human life," it was therefore *redefining* not only our "liberty," but a large part of what it means to be American, too. The Justices were keenly aware that they were doing so; in fact, they were consciously trying to do so. For in the *Casey* opinion the Justices proclaimed that Americans' "belief in themselves" as a law-abiding people "is not readily separable from their understanding of the Court invested with the authority to decide their constitutional cases and speak before all others for their constitutional ideals. If the Court's legitimacy should be undermined, then, so would the country be in its very ability to see itself through its constitutional ideals." The Justices went so far as to liken the Constitution to a "covenant" of which they were the keepers: "[w]e accept our responsibility not to retreat from interpreting the full meaning of the covenant in light of all of our precedents. We invoke it once again to define the freedom guaranteed by the Constitution's own promise, the promise of liberty."

If these bold judicial declarations were hubristic overreaches, this book would not be needed. Alas, the now infamous *Casey* "Mystery Passage" synthesized a full generation of prior Court holdings on subjects as important as religion in public life, religious liberty, marriage and family, having and raising children, education, and sexual morality. "These matters," the Justices wrote in 1992, "involving the most intimate and personal choices a person may make in a lifetime, choices central to personal dignity and autonomy, are central to the liberty protected by the Fourteenth Amendment."[1]

It has been another full generation since. By now Americans have exhausted the cultural capital stored up by the believing Christians and Jews who came before them, and which muffled the effects of the new age heralded by *Casey*. The Greatest Generation is now nearly gone; very few of them survive. Their offspring, the baby-boomers who rebelled against their elders, are retired or retiring. America is being run by persons who did not know the world before 1968. More than a half-century into great social upheaval, we know what it is like to ride bareback across the open range of human egotism, desire, and fantasy, unconstrained by the Decalogue and other objective moral truths.

Lamentations abound. Archbishop Charles Chaput's *Strangers in a*

---

1   Some perceptive observers (including my Notre Dame colleague Patrick Deneen, in his fine book *Why Liberalism Failed*) think that they see the origins, or the embryonic nucleus, of this developing debacle in the Founding. I rather think it is sufficient to recognize that the radical subjectivism of the Mystery Passage is what happens when a Christian society secularizes. At various points in this book I shall explain further what I mean by "post-Christian" society and why I think it is the predictable devolution of a secularizing Christian society, with a special *caveat* that what is usually called "liberal Christianity", with its elevation of the "pastoral" and "experiential" and deep interior "conversion" over "dogma" and moral "rules", functions as midwife of the transition.

I leave the large questions of *why* and *how* our society secularized to another book, one which won't be written by me.

Strange Land (2017) frankly describes the cultural ruins surrounding us, while retaining a proper Christian hope. R.R. Reno's *Resurrecting the Idea of a Christian Society* (2016) and Anthony Esolen's *Out of the Ashes: Rebuilding American Cultures* (2017) are fine complements to Chaput's sobering reflections. In his *The Benedict Option* (2017), Rod Dreher does *not* (as some think he does, and as the title might suggest) counsel withdrawal from the world of politics and law, as if becoming like the Amish was the only way to play on. Dreher does, however, frankly describe a degraded anti-Christian culture. He offers dire warnings about the prospects of living a Christian life without cultivating a detached, subculturalist attitude toward the mainstream of American life. In its 2019 document "Male and Female He Created Them," the Vatican's Congregation for Catholic Education wrote that the "transformation of social and interpersonal relationships has often waved the 'flag of freedom,' but it has, in reality, brought spiritual and material devastation to countless human beings."

This book is mostly about the law of civil liberties. But its impetus is not legal. Its subject is broader than anything the Supreme Court is up to. The *Casey* doctrine about liberty's core is mistaken as a matter of constitutional interpretation. The precedents which it synthesized and which it subsequently spawned are also misbegotten. In the chapters which follow we shall see how some of these misguided doctrines about civil liberties should be corrected. But the principal concern of this book is neither doctrinal nor historical. It is an argument to restore moral truth as the foundation of our law of civil liberties, because doing so is one productive response to the crisis of living a Christian life in our time.

This book calls for frankly recognizing that our law of civil liberties has been co-opted by the moral subjectivism expressed by the Mystery Passage. Perhaps any reader who follows current events knows the challenges faced by wedding vendors driven from the marketplace; Christian adoption agencies cut off from government contracts; medical professionals threatened with sanctions for refusing to participate in abortions; a few parents whose children are taken away because they will not go along with the child's delusion that he is really a she: all these stories (and more like them) are staples of popular media.

At first glance the Mystery Passage might seem to preserve a silent and unoberservable sphere of the mind, where imagination may run free as the wind. But it is more than that, for what the mind conceives the person is today entitled to express, and to actualize. At second glance the Mystery Passage might seem to preserve a zone of non-interference, a do-not-disturb private realm where the expressive individual may act out without being molested by others. But it is more than that. The corollary of *Casey's* radical autonomy is no longer (if it ever was) non-interference. It now entails a community-wide duty to "affirm" the imagined world of another person out of "respect" for the person whose world it is. By 2015 social "recognition" was part of what it meant to have the "liberty" of self-definition. This crucial addition to the *Casey* Mystery Passage is the other half of the "identity politics" diptych which suffuses our culture and law. The escutcheon of today's "liberty" carries the image of Indiana public-school teacher John Kluge, who was fired for refusing to go along with his employer's forced affirmation policy for "transgendered" students. Kluge would not embrace a lie. It is not that cases like Kluge's are already common. But they will be, because the new order of civil liberties leads exactly to his dismissal.

In these pages I shall try to show that even all these serious injustices are just the surface manifestations of a seismic shift across our whole culture, a change in social worldviews transpiring around us which has now become part of the cultural air that we breathe.

Culture is much more than museums and art fairs and musicals. Culture is comprised more importantly of large social institutions and practices: marriage, religion, educational systems, and public morality. It is, even more broadly, the patterns of meaning and value that people living in any community share. Culture has great purchase upon persons' hearts and minds and on the choices that bear upon their moral well-being.

Although the civil law does not occupy our whole social life, since *Casey* it has penetrated and shaped much more of our lives than it ever did before. This infiltration is not just regulatory; that is, normative of our behavior. Civil law has in most places at most times been a powerful educative force, a great teacher as well as an efficient monitor. In *both* respects combined – as monitor and as teacher – the civil law in our country powerfully shapes culture. Because culture so powerfully shapes our understanding of what is truly worthwhile, as well as practical opportunities for realizing what is truly good, culture shapes *us*.

The law does not shape us only by setting up green lights and red lights. It does that sometimes, by prohibiting some acts and requiring others. The law also shapes us by creating incentives and disincentives. Permitted acts can be discouraged by taxes and burdensome regulations. Others can be encouraged and even subsidized. But the law can and does shape us more powerfully, yet more subtly, by shaping the *culture* in which we live. The law today powerfully shapes the social understandings, practices, and meanings of the good life that constitute our common culture.

These are not necessary truths about law. They are not axioms of social theory or political science. The relationship between civil law and culture in any society is rather a contingent matter. In some places, the law has little or no purchase upon the local culture. Sometimes the government is too weak to matter. (Think of failing states in the Third World.) Sometimes the government is too remote to matter. ("God bless the czar and keep him…far away from us!" was the rabbi's prayer in *Fiddler on the Roof*.) Sometimes the government has no moral authority. (Consider the Communist regime in Poland before 1989.) Sometimes folk customs, tribal ways, and religious norms of conduct are enough to keep a community on track. Civil law might then be an afterthought. (Think of all of the above.)

Francis Cardinal George aptly stated that "law has peculiar and unique cultural functions in American society." In a lecture delivered at Notre Dame Law School in 2002 Cardinal George observed that

> The many components of our culture are largely united by law, not by blood, not by race, not by religion, not even by language, but by law. It's the one principal cultural component we all have in common. … [L]aw is more important in teaching or instructing us than it is in directing us. … [O]ne must therefore ask how it is that law functions as a cultural carrier in [this country], and what does that mean for cultural institutions that are

---

2   "Law and Culture in the United States", 48 *The American Journal of Jurisprudence* 131 (2003).

universal [i.e., objective, natural] but that are qualified by law: marriage, family [and others].[2]

The Supreme Court itself recognized this profound capacity of positive law to shape a culture and thereby to shape us. When it affirmed the central holding of *Roe v. Wade* in 1992 in *Planned Parenthood v. Casey,* the Justices said that "[a]n entire generation has come of age free to assume *Roe's* concept of liberty in defining the capacity of women to act in society, and to make reproductive decisions." With what effect? "[F]or two decades … people have organized intimate relationships and made choices that define their views of themselves and their places in society, in reliance on the availability of abortion in the event that contraception should fail. The ability of women to participate equally in the economic and social life of the Nation has been facilitated by their ability to control their reproductive lives."

Note well: *Casey* was not talking mainly about the millions of women who have had abortions. The *Casey* Court was talking instead about how *Roe* altered the psychology and self-understanding, the dreams and potential achievements, of every woman. *All* women allegedly benefitted from the control over their bodies which abortion assertedly gave them. This "reproductive freedom" is the linchpin of women's freedom and equality – or so abortion advocates persistently assert.

Reconstituting civil liberties in order to build a culture conducive to upright living is work with a claim upon everyone's attention. Although one motivation and one anticipated benefit of grounding civil liberties in moral truth has to do with Christian living – and that is value enough in itself – the project is not sectarian or parochial. Far from it. A properly founded and guided system of civil liberties is an enormous good for everyone. It is a fundamental component of the true common good of any political society, including ours. Nonetheless, in America today, the effort will have to be led by faithful Catholics.

The way forward looks into uncharted terrain. The Catholic Church has a lot of experience evangelizing worlds previously untouched by the Gospel. It has some experience (re)evangelizing peoples whose faith has been (or is being) forcibly suppressed by totalitarian regimes. But the Church has little experience with the dilemma expressed by the sub-titles of Chaput's and Dreher's books: *Living the Catholic Faith in a Post-Christian World* and *A Strategy for Christians in a Post-Christian Nation,* respectively.

One reason why Catholics must serve as the vanguard is that the Church's social teaching presents the essential corrective clearly and cogently. Thirteen months after *Casey*, a radically different definition of "liberty" was put on offer in Rome. Occasioned not by the Mystery Passage as such but by the contemporary embrace, even by Catholics, of "proportionalist" and (less so) of subjectivist moral theories, Pope John Paull II on August 6, 1993, affirmed in the encyclical letter *Veritatis splendor* that genuine freedom could not be understood save as oriented to and in service to objective moral truth. The Holy Father introduced the letter proclaiming: "Truth enlightens man's intelligence and shapes his freedom." Truth is an essential part of any proper use of freedom and is in fact the grounds of individuality: "[O]nly by obedience to universal moral norms does man find full confirmation of his personal uniqueness and the possibility of authentic moral growth. For this very reason, this service is also directed to *all mankind:* it is not only for individuals but *also for the community, for society as such.*" (VS 96; emphasis added).

The Pope in VS did not therefore speak only about how individuals should understand their own freedom when governing their particular choices, as if one should construct one's own moral universe as if God sanctioned an objective moral law. In addition to that, he articulated the foundation of Catholic *social* teaching:

> *When it is a matter of the moral norms prohibiting intrinsic evil, there are no privileges or exceptions for anyone.* It makes no difference whether one is the master of the world or the "poorest of the poor" on the face of the earth. Before the demands of morality, we are all absolutely equal. [Emphasis in the original]

In respect of moral absolutes – or what might better be called *exceptionless negative moral norms*, such as torture, rape, and intentional killing, which are *never* morally permissible – there is *one* morality, a singular foundation of moral truths such as those found in the Decalogue, which governs everyone's choices in every sphere of human life. Make no mistake about it: "Civil authorities ... never have authority to violate the fundamental and inalienable rights of the human person." "Even though intentions may sometimes be good, and circumstances frequently difficult, civil authorities and particular individuals never have authority to violate the fundamental and inalienable rights of the human person."[3]

The unicity of morality's import is not limited to the very important office of obliging even the "master of the world" to submit to moral truth. In VS 97 Pope John Paul II wrote that the "commandments of the second table of the Decalogue in particular – those which Jesus quoted to the young man of the Gospel 9cf. Mt. 19:19) – constitute the indispensable rules of all social life." The exceptionless moral prohibitions of adultery, intentional killing, theft, and lying represent "the unshakable foundation and solid guarantee of a just and peaceful human coexistence, and hence of genuine democracy, which can come into being and develop only on the basis of the equality of all its members, who possess common rights and duties." As Pope John Paul II said, "[i]n the end, only a morality which acknowledges certain norms as valid *always and for everyone, with no exception,* can guarantee the ethical foundation of social coexistence, both on the national and international levels."

---

3   This powerful statement of the unicity of morality synthesized decades of doctrinal indications. Just looking at the last hundred years or so we see in *Quas primas* (1925): " ... truly the whole of mankind is subject to the power of Jesus Christ." Nor is there any difference in this matter between the individual and the family or the State; for all men, whether collectively or individually, are under the dominion of Christ."

Pope Pius XI made his relevant meaning clearer in 1937, in his Encyclical *Mit brennender Sorge*, which denounced among other evils National Socialism. Sec. 10: "God, this Sovereign Master, has issued commandments whose value is independent of time and space, country and race. As God's sun shines on every human face so His law knows neither privilege nor exception. Rulers and subjects, crowned and uncrowned, rich and poor are equally subject to His word ..."

The unity of morality is expressed later by Saint John XXIII in *Pacem in Terris* (1963) secs. 80-81: "The same law of nature that governs the life and conduct of individuals must also regulate the relations of political communities with one another. ... political leaders ... are bound by the natural law, which is the rule that governs all moral conduct, and they have no authority to depart from its slightest precepts."

Pope John Paul and the tradition for which he speaks point the way forward. The first seven chapters of this book engage the most contentious civil liberties, including religious freedom, marriage and family, abortion, sex discrimination, and access of "transgendered" students to bathrooms (and other intimate facilities) reserved to the opposite sex, albeit also of the sex which the student imagines to be his or her own. These chapters show that the soundest *legal* arguments against the champions of radical "autonomy" are based squarely upon moral truth and, on the questions of when people begin and the bases for ascertaining anyone's sex (male or female), in metaphysical truth as well.

This book of essays is not a call to meet legal arguments rooted in the contemporary existentialist search for personal "identity" with quotations from papal documents or from Scripture. It is not a call to abandon more restricted and technical legal arguments in civil liberty cases; that species of reasoning and rhetoric remains invaluable. It is a call to renew the cultural and legal struggle to found our civil liberties upon moral truth.

The final three chapters turn specifically to Catholics' repertoire for the coming battle. These chapters examine the laity's vocation to redeem the temporal order, the future of Catholic institutional ministries generally, and specifically of Catholic higher education.

The effort will make Catholics "Unquiet Americans." They will be unquiet *Americans* because they will be performing a patriotic duty, and because they will be engaged in an effort to remove from civil liberties law an excrescence which has grievously disfigured the American tradition. They will be *unquiet* Americans because it has always been an article of their civic faith that, notwithstanding the calumnies and suspicions of many of their countrymen, there was no basic incompatibility between faithful devotion to the true Church and full loyalty to the United States. One could be both a good Catholic and a good American, and millions of Catholics went to their graves – often enough on foreign fields of battle – firmly convinced that they had been. Catholics have been "outsiders" in some significant ways through much of their sojourn on these shores. But if America's Catholics answer *this* call to serve their countrymen and their country's common good, they will be speaking truth to power in an unaccustomed way. They will be made to suffer insult and recrimination for doing so.

****

A decent respect for the reader as well as for the strength of the argument of this book require a straight-on critique of the Mystery Passage, considered just as a proposal about the meaning and value of individual's freedom. That critique, substantially borrowed from a published essay of mine ("Three Liberal – But Mistaken – Arguments for Same-sex Marriage," published in the 2008 volume of the *South Texas Law Review*), is Appendix 1. Some parts of other chapters have appeared in previous publications. But everything in the book has been either written or revised for this publication.

I have purposefully kept footnotes and other more strictly scholarly apparatus to a bare minimum, in order to enhance readability for a wide audience.

Chapter One
The Future of Religious Liberty

Religious liberty was planted in America by Protestants working on distinctively Protestant soil. Their handiwork was nonetheless supple enough to absorb the shock of Roman Catholicism during the nineteenth century, and to survive the death of the "implicit" Protestant establishment at the turn of the twentieth. By the end of World War II American religious liberty incorporated Judaism into the new "tri-faith" America; then, the term "Judeo-Christian tradition" was introduced into our national vocabulary to indicate this successful merger, or melding, of biblical religions. By that time, too, American Christianity had balkanized into some 250 sects, according to one Supreme Court Justice's estimate; another Justice (Robert Jackson) quaintly observed in 1944 that *"[s]cores of sects flourish in this country by teaching what to me are queer notions."* These odd groups included Jehovah's Witnesses, who characteristically believed in no human government; God' sovereignty over the universe was undivided. They refused to salute the flag, and they bitterly denounced Catholics. Yet these Witnesses won signal religious liberty victories in the Supreme Court during the 1940s, in cases where they did *these things!* In the 1960s American religious liberty confronted, and renewed itself by digesting, rugged religious individualism. Existentialists who doubted God, and other loners who professed no creed and belonged to no sect, won Supreme Court victories for religious liberty.

Each of these encounters left its mark: religious liberty changed and grew stronger and more inclusive, even as America experienced, in addition to all the challenges just described, profound secularization through the whole twentieth century. Religious liberty weathered that challenge, too, proving itself a most resilient "first freedom."

It is therefore more than remarkable that, for the first time in American history, it recently became respectable to publicly oppose religious liberty and its supreme value in our polity. This unprecedented turn is ominous. It will not only diminish our constitutional law. It will remap our common life, for religious liberty has always been not only a strategic linchpin of our panoply of civil liberties but also an anchor of our whole political culture, a defining feature of America as "the land of the free."

To be sure, Americans in the past often opposed *particular* claims of religious liberty – of Latter-Day Saints concerning polygamy, for example, or of Catholics who resisted Protestant observances in public school rooms, or of Native-American parents claiming their rightful authority to direct the religious upbringing of their children, when public authorities would force their children to attend distant special schools in order to more efficiently assimilate them. In none of these past episodes or in the often-heated debates about them did anyone publicly question the great and general value of religious liberty itself.

What is happening now is different. Opposition back then was to a specific activity of a particular religious group, say, to LDS plural marriages. What is happening now is happening to religion across a broader front of issues. The brunt of the new hostility to religious liberty is not being born by religious minorities, either. Christians who adhere to what was until recently America's common morality are instead its chief victims. Besides, when Mormons and Catholics and Indians found themselves on the losing side, no one associated religious liberty itself with unjust discrimination, or with "demeaning" anyone's "dignity," much less with hatred and bigotry. Now, many do. And the percentages of Americans who belong to some sort of religious body, or even say that they believe in God, are at all-time lows. The rates of disassociation from religion and of outright atheism among the young are shockingly high.

I

Same-sex wedding vendor cases, most prominently including the continuing saga of *Masterpiece Cakeshop*, constitute the most prominent front of the present challenge to our "first freedom." But the threat is much broader, comprehensive, and grave than even that tranche of troubling cases suggests. The trajectory upon which *Casey* launched our "liberty" has altered the course of religious freedom more than any other civil liberty. It is not so much that religious freedom is being increasingly limited by ever-greater valuation of competing liberties, such as those associated with reproduction. It is rather that religious liberty is on the road to extinction.

Someone might be thinking that this means that sexual freedom, most keenly for those (like homosexuals and lesbians) who have suffered some unfair discrimination for their sexual orientations, is strong enough to suppress religious liberty. On this view, there is no *broader* or *deeper* threat – the explanation for what is happening does not go beyond the libido. Apart from sex, religious liberty is doing well.

Not so. Consider for example that the federal Religious Freedom Restoration Act was a welcome, bipartisan measure that has served religious liberty well. It passed unanimously in the House of Representatives; there were just three dissenting votes in the Senate – in 1993! Then Congressman (now Senator) Chuck Schumer introduced it in the House of Representatives; liberal lion Ted Kennedy introduced it in the Senate. I noticed the rebellion against sexual morality while I was in high school; how could any teenage boy not notice the cleavage and innuendo even on prime-time television? And I discovered that college life was in full debauch when I enrolled at Cornell in 1972.

The sexual revolution may be a necessary part of the gale-force headwind buffeting religious liberty. But sexual freedom is not nearly sufficient to present an existential threat. Only the more sweeping transformation of the meaning of liberty – from choices between what is good and what is evil on a path to perfecting oneself, to inventive self-expression for the sake of an alleged "authenticity" – could menace religious freedom itself. By redefining and revaluing *all* "liberty," our culture and our law have loosed a Trojan Horse within the walls of our "first freedom."

Today's open opposition to religious liberty is the front of a broad movement of thought and action. The Obama Administration's stance in the 2012 Supreme Court case about the "ministerial exception" to employment discrimination laws – *EEOC v. Hosanna-Tabor* – is a pristine illustration of the Trojan Horse at work. That case pertained to the civil liberty of churches to conduct their internal affairs free of government interference. There was then at hand a long line of solid constitutional precedents affirming a substantial "autonomy," rooted in the great and distinctive value of religion and churches to persons' flourishing and to the common weal. The United States nonetheless boldly declared in *Hosanna-Tabor* that religion should have *no* "special" – that is, no distinct or favorable – constitutional or legal status!

The Administration's startling submission was that churches do have rights – the same rights (no more and no less) than any other ideological associations. The Lutheran Church which was party to *Hosanna-Tabor*, for example, would enjoy the same prerogatives as do the Boy Scouts and the Rotary Club and the Democratic Party. The Court confidently rejected the Administration's position, observing that there is, after all, "special" mention of religion in the Free Exercise Clause.

Indeed. But the Obama Lawyers simply expressed the logic of religious liberty in our emerging culture of self-invention. They overreached in 2012. The question is whether their argument will ring true to the Supreme Court in, say, 2025.

In the minds and hearts of many people today, and in the experience of extraordinarily large numbers of those who are under thirty years old, "religion" comprises the deeper, more contemplative aspects of an encompassing project of creative self-definition. It is the spiritual component of one's "identity" or personal "brand." What churches and other purveyors of religious services offer is processed and evaluated by the expressive self according to experiential metrics: What does (could?) that liturgy do for me? How does it make me feel? Is it empowering? Or does it bring me "down"? The whole transaction is grounded in non-religious indices of personal well-being and non-moral, psychological values.

The foundation of value here is not the correspondence of any religion's content to what there is – seen and unseen. The value of religion lies not in the truth about anyone's obligations to a greater-than-human source of meaning and value. The metric of worth is a certain authenticity, that is, one's subjective sense of one's own deepest self. Religion is about personal *identity*. It is not about any reality larger than that.

In most academic legal commentary, in much law, and to a significant extent in the minds of many people, religious acts have the same dignity and value as do other acts by which persons express and actualize their deepest selves, desires, or self-defining thoughts and emotions. The supreme and perhaps only universal value here is authenticity and thus "identity."

As John Finnis aptly observed, religion's "status and immunities are as instances…of the only really basic human good, the only intrinsically worthwhile end at stake, setting for oneself one's stance in the world." Religion is, in other words, a component of many persons' identity and a source of societal diversity. An English law lord (named Law) gave thematic expression to this development in a recent case when he denied relief to a Christian relationship counselor who could not endorse the same-sex acts of his potential clients. The counselor's refusal was a prima facie case of sexual-orientation discrimination. She sought an exception rooted in ambient legal norms of religious liberty. Lord Law declared that any exemption on religious grounds would be "unprincipled." He reasoned that it would "give effect to the force of subjective opinion" (read: religion) and thus could not "advance the general good on objective grounds."

Consider these evidences of promiscuous interbreeding between the Mystery Passage "identity" project and religious liberty. Justice Kennedy in *Hobby Lobby* said that free exercise is "essential" to preserving the "dignity" of those who choose to "striv[e] for a self-definition shaped by their religious precepts." This same liberty anchors his opinion for the *Obergefell* Court: "The right to marry thus dignifies couples who 'wish to define themselves by their commitment to each other.'" In *Casey* the joint opinion writers (including Justice Kennedy) declared that a woman's abortion decision "originate[s] in the zone of conscience and belief" and must be settled by "her own conception of her spiritual imperatives."

Another leading American – then-Senator Barack Obama – described religion as each one's "narrative arc," which "relieve[s] a chronic loneliness, …an assurance that somebody out there cares about them, is listening to them – that they are not just destined to travel down that long highway towards nothingness." This religion sounds much like *Obergefell's* vision of marriage, which Justice Kennedy asserted "responds to the universal fear that a lonely person might call out only to find no one there."

II

Religious liberty in the new dispensation is really one subdivision, or set of exercises, of the one Great Liberty, given authoritative expression in *Planned Parenthood v. Casey*: "At the heart of liberty is the right to define one's own concept of existence, of meaning, of the universe, and of the mystery of human life." The Mystery Passage seems to be a *characteristically* post-Christian phenomenon. Where a culture has been decisively shaped by Christianity, that religion's supreme commitment to each individual's responsibility for his eternal destiny makes the post-Christian transformation of that culture into one of group identity unlikely. Because of the First Commandment, a Christian culture will eliminate rival gods and disenchant nature and the cosmos. Some superstition and pantheistic remnants might survive, usually in syncretistic fashion. Christianity's distinctive rejection of divine absolutism, in favor of its unique understanding that God adopts human persons into his family through Baptism and calls persons to a kind of friendship and collaboration, makes authoritarian religious alternatives (or successors) to Christianity incredible.

In a political culture characterized by limited government and individual rights, the constitutional tradition makes collapse into anything like state-worship nearly impossible (which is not to say that *statism* is improbable). Plainly put: in a Christian culture the only possible sources of meaning and value for human beings are either God or the choosing and acting human person himself. Once God is removed from the scene, or as soon as God becomes a forgiving life coach, the only source of value is the individual. When American constitutional law imagined a secular America, it was only a matter of time before religion would become an individualized, noncognitive enterprise. Then religious liberty would inevitably collapse into a freedom to manifest one's personal identity, including (for many) an idiosyncratic spiritual brand.

Now, it is true that religions *include* subjective experiences, as well as stories and prescriptions that are historical and contingent and, in that way, arbitrary. But religions are much more than that. They are more or less reasonable accounts of reality in all of its breadth, including its furthest reaches, visible and invisible. The indispensable criterion of a religion's value is whether it is *true*. The central value of religious liberty is the protection it offers to those who seek the truth about the cosmos and who resolve to live their lives in accord with what they believe to be the truth about all that there is. Sever it from this fountainhead in the search, guided by reason, for the truth about all that there is, and religious liberty will wither and eventually disappear.

III

The effects of this transformation are not limited to some notional "private sphere" of life. The repercussions are powerful. They course outward and remap our whole social world. The boundary lines on the new chart divide human activity into two basic realms. The first is "public" life, defined expansively to include not only law and political affairs but commercial and social intercourse too. This space is to be governed by a secular orthodoxy from which only mental reservation is permitted. As Justice Alito wrote in *Obergefell*: "those who cling to the old beliefs will be able to whisper their thoughts in the recesses of their own homes."

In the public realm religion may supply motivation for some people, and a common stock of phrases and images for many more. But religion may not supply cognizable reasons or plausible arguments for public policy. The reason why not is simple enough – It lies in the nature of religion and religious belief. In a 2006 talk then-Senator Obama explained how "[d]emocracy demands that the religiously motivated translate their concerns into universal...values." The reasons were two: religion, he said, does not allow for compromise, and it is not subject to argument or amenable to reason. Religion is, in other words, irrational, non-cognitive, utterly subjective. "To base one's life on such uncompromising commitments may be sublime, but to base our policy making on such commitments would be a dangerous thing."

In one especially telling wedding-vendor case, that of *Elane Photography v. Willock*, the New Mexico Supreme Court ruled in favor of a lesbian couple who asserted that, under the state law outlawing discrimination on grounds of sexual orientation in all "public accommodations," a wedding photographer was bound to shoot video at their "commitment ceremony." Concurring in that result, Justice Bosson recognized that the photographers – the Huguenins – acted out of a sincere Christian belief that the ceremony celebrated an immoral sexual relationship and that memorializing it in pictures made them complicit in the immorality. Justice Bosson wrote, tellingly, that the Huguenins are "free to think, to say, to believe, as they wish; they may pray to the God of their choice and follow these commandments in their personal lives." In the world of "the marketplace, of commerce, of public accommodation," they must "compromise." They "must channel their conduct, not their beliefs, so as to leave space for other Americans who believe something different." They must adhere to the "glue which holds us together as a nation, the tolerance that lubricates the varied moving parts of us as a people." This is "the price of citizenship."

IV

Here is a snapshot of the dynamic described in the preceding two sections in action. It is a picture of how what we could usefully call *identity politics* poses an especially great threat to religious liberty.

One is that what believers invariably understand themselves to be doing – which is steering clear of immoral involvement in the bad conduct of another person – is by force of reconceptualization replaced with a substitute, namely the personal status or "identity" of some putative victim, that is, of a person self-identifying or presenting as a member of a supposedly vulnerable group.

Thus, a wedding vendor's refusal to supply *anyone*, straight or "gay," with a cake or flowers for celebrating an ersatz marriage is re-conceptualized as discrimination by him or her against "gay" customers. Innkeepers who refuse to rent to fornicators are charged with discriminating on grounds of marital status. Employers who cannot conscientiously distribute contraceptives discriminate against women. Teenagers who refuse to disrobe in the presence of a member of the opposite sex (albeit one assertedly suffering from gender dysphoria) demean that person's self-understanding.

Compounding this first error is the prevalent notion that where public authority recognizes the religious liberty of a wedding vendor, the state puts its own "imprimatur" on that person's allegedly unjust discrimination, and even on the normative premise underlying the vendor's conscientious refusal, namely, the truth that marriage between two men or two women is impossible.

This whole "imprimatur" idea is hogwash, cooked up for the purpose of bludgeoning those who resist the new orthodoxy about sex and marriage. Besides, no one ever suggested that, when the Jehovah's Witnesses secured their right not to salute the flag, the Court was endorsing their denial of

United States sovereignty in favor of God's undivided sovereignty. Lawmakers who recognize Amish claims about limited schooling do not thereby ratify Old Order Anabaptist beliefs. You do not profess, endorse, ratify, or show the slightest sympathy with Native American beliefs by supporting their right of access to peyote-infused rituals. And so on. The "imprimatur" claim is jerry-rigged to make the facts of these cases fit an identity politics morality tale.

A third error builds upon the first two. Often styled as "dignitary" harm, the idea seems to be that when one is refused a service due to the provider's moral qualms about activities of yours that you are inviting him to participate in or assist, one's person or identity is "demeaned" and one's "dignity" is attacked.

There are many mistakes in this line of thought. One mistake is about dignity itself, which has to do with the inherent qualities of persons which make them rights-bearers and worthy of respect. "Dignity" properly understood is not prone to be compromised by others' bad behavior.

Let's set that miscue aside. It is ever more apparent that, in this context, we are really talking about *perceived* insult, about a same-sex couple's *feeling* that they have been humiliated or demeaned, even though no word has been spoken, no gesture made, that means anything more than, "It is against my conscience to participate." Then again, we are securely in the realm of identity politics, where self-esteem – at least for those who happen to be in favor – rules the day.

The Supreme Court's same-sex "marriage" decision, *Obergefell v. Hodges,* traffics in this same identity-politics. The opening sentence of that opinion introduces a concept of liberty that "includes…[the] right[] of persons within a lawful realm to define and express their identity." The center of gravity in *Obergefell* is communal affirmation of each person's intimate and self-defining choice of a companion to ward off "the universal fear that a lonely person call out only to find no one there." Indeed, if you deleted from the majority opinion the complex of thoughts about "identity" (which could be well summarized thus: the purpose of marriage law is to communicate the whole community's affirmation of the same-sex couple's self-defining choice to marry and thereby to avoid "demeaning" or "humiliating" them), there would not be a syllable of justification left in it.

V

The wedding vendor cases are surely worth the attention that so many people give them. They have become the nodal point of hostile contact between competing worldviews. The stakes are indeed high. The litigated outcomes have been mostly unfortunate; the vendors lose more often than they win. Worse, one can safely speculate that countless people like Jack Phillips (the proprietor of Masterpiece Cakeshop and protagonist of the Supreme Court case of that name) do not fight back as he did. Many vendors no doubt quietly cave in to the unjust demands of the state. A few might instead quietly leave the trade altogether. It is surely a cause worth fighting for.

Someone might object to the argument of this chapter: that nothing short of a radical strategy could possibly preserve religious liberty for our posterity. Many genuine friends of real religious liberty instead stress the wisdom, if not the necessity, of working *within* the parameters of thought and argument presently on offer. They resist calls for a breakout of religion into the public realm or an overhaul of what the culture (and especially young people) think religion is. They would seek instead fairer treatment of religion as one source among many of private edification or personal identity. Many of these friends are litigators and political strategists with professional obligations to seek success on a one-off basis, either for a particular client or in order to win the next vote.

Tactical victory is certainly preferable to tactical defeat. But tactics are suited to small-unit engagements. The argument of this chapter is that fighting it out along a line drawn in our constitutional law nearly four-score years ago can do no more than slow down the pace of defeat. Religious liberty is in the maws of a great cultural shift. Nothing less than radical strategic action has any chance of preserving religious liberty beyond the foreseeable future.

A broader and deeper foundation is needed, too, because these wedding vendor cases are just the tip of the iceberg. They do not touch the more difficult challenge of *Obergefell*, which is not about working with same-sex *weddings* but about living with same-sex *marriages*. No one needs legal permission to decline an invitation to the wedding of two men or two women. Very few of us will even be asked to do the flowers at one. We can more or less effectively steer clear of same-sex nuptials, no matter what the law is.

But all of us have to face – and will face for the rest of our days – the challenge of what to do about the two civilly married men who apply to live in your co-op, or who want you to take their family portrait, or who will soon join your school's Parent Teacher Association, or who will eventually come to you for marital counselling. Same-sex "weddings" are the stuff of save-the-date and a precise GPS location. Same-sex marriage is everywhere, all of the time. One cannot hide from it.

People have had to live with irregular sexual relationships since the dawn of time. But legalized same-sex marriage is different than anything that has plagued societies before. For one thing, such relationships are about as distant from real marriage as any relationship could be. Second, recognizing the sexual consortium of two men or two women as marriages settles conclusively that marriage as such is *sterile*. (Indeed, that was the fundamental issue at stake in the whole fight over same-sex marriage.) Third, there are no fig leaves available to obscure or fudge the manifest immorality, and parody of marriage, presented by same-sex relationships. An opposite-sex couple in a bad marriage is not detectable as such at a glance. A merely cohabiting man and woman will not be wearing wedding rings and will not expect to be addressed as if they are spouses. And in decades and centuries past, those in irregular sexual relationships rarely demanded that their liaisons be treated as respectable and good, much less on a par with the procreative marriages of man and woman.

The everyday challenge of legalized same-sex "marriage" is whether those who hold the "decent and honorable religious" conviction that it is impossible for two persons of the same sex to marry will be accorded the legal and social space needed in order to live in accord with our convictions. The question at hand is whether we will instead be forced to contradict our convictions in word and deed, day in and day out. Chief Justice Roberts wrote in *Obergefell*:

> Hard questions arise when people of faith exercise religion in ways that may be seen to conflict with the new right to same-sex marriage – when, for example, a religious college provides married student housing only to opposite-sex married couples, or a religious adoption agency declines to place children with same-sex married couples.

Conclusion

Friends of religious liberty *must* yank its subject matter out of the nest of subjectivity and irrationality to which it has been consigned by those who prize the "freedom" of the Mystery Passage. These friends must reconnect religion and truth. Not with "truth," as if religious convictions might have a non-cognitive validity, as revisable human articulations of seemingly compelling personal experiences – the "truth" of poetry, or of good sex. Religions rather should be judged by the metrics we predicate of other worldviews, of rival accounts of the way the cosmos really is, and is constituted, and where it is all heading.

This reconnection must be achieved by and through reason, as the following two chapters explore.

Chapter 2
Religious Liberty and Moral Truth

Among the greatest achievements of America's founders was establishing religious liberty upon religious truth. They were, almost to the last one, Protestants. A few were wobbly in faith. But on the whole the founding generation's Christian beliefs were strong and enduring. Their foundation for religious liberty nevertheless included a significant portion of what might best be described as "natural theology," or those truths about the Supreme Being and its relationship to creation and to humankind that are available to the inquiring mind unaided by revelation.

The founders did not seek nor value freedom *from* religion. That idea would have struck them all as preposterous, for atheism was not then a publicly respectable position and – as we shall see – they regarded organized religion as the bulwark of the republic. Religious liberty was certainly not rooted in the rootless freedom of self-invention we examined in the last chapter. That sort of rank voluntarism was scarcely conceivable to the founders and, in any event, they regarded the morality of the Decalogue as an essential prop of their experiment in liberty.

Our tradition of religious liberty is founded in convictions such as those expressed by James Madison, our fourth President and a moving force behind the enactment of our Bill of Rights. The Supreme Court in 1947 stamped Madison's *Memorial and Remonstrance*, written in 1786 during the course of a Virginia debate over state support of religion teachers, as the *Magna Carta* of religious liberty in America. Madison's ode to religious freedom listed, as the first of fifteen grounds for opposing support of compulsory assessments, that "religion or the duty which we owe to our Creator and the Manner of discharging it, can be directed only by reason and conviction, not by force or violence." This Madison affirmed, not as a hypothesis or as the lesson of experience or as the special deliverance of the distinctively political reflection or reason, but as *true.*

The founders promoted freedom of religion not only for the sake of religion, and for the religious well-being of persons. The founders promoted religious freedom for the sake of the polity, too. They were utterly convinced that religion was an essential support of free government, and for that reason religion and the free adherence to it should be duly encouraged by public authority. "Of all the dispositions and habits which lead to political prosperity, Religion and Morality are indispensable supports," Washington said in his Farewell Address. "And let us with caution indulge the supposition, that morality can be maintained without Religion. Whatever may be conceded of the influence of refined education on minds of peculiar structure; reason and experience both forbid us to expect that national morality can prevail in exclusion of religious principle. John Adams thought that "religion and virtue" were the only foundations not only of republicanism "but of social felicity under all governments and in all the combinations of human society." Jefferson feared for a future America shorn of Christian morality.

Even Baptists' hostility to New England's legally supported orthodoxy did not contradict these cautions. Baptist Reverend Isaac Backus was perhaps the most influential member of the Protestant clergy during the founding years. He opined that religion "keeps alive the vest sense of moral obligation . . . The fear and reverence of God and the terrors of eternity are the most powerful restrains upon the mind of men. And hence it is of special importance in a free government, the spirit of which being always friendly to the sacred rights of conscience; it will hold up the Gospel as the great rule of faith and practice."

Thomas Jefferson, to whom Christianity was both the most sublime and the most perverse system known to the world, noted in 1781 that American liberty depended on a popular perception that it was the gift of God and thought it politically beneficial if Americans privately decided that there was "only one God, and he all perfect" and that there was a future state of rewards and punishments. At about the same time, he drafted a bill for the Virginia Assembly authorizing punishment of ministers who failed to preach sermons at the legislature's command. Later, President Jefferson negotiated a treaty with the Kaskaskia Indians the terms of which included government provision of Catholic missionaries to the tribe.

The prevailing picture now is quite different. Almost no one any more contends that public well-being depends essentially upon private piety. And how could it, where religion is no longer about bringing one's choices and actions into line with moral and religious truth? Religious liberty is no longer really our "first freedom." How could it be, when "religion" is deemed irrational and has been absorbed into the revelries of the solipsistic individual? *Then*, republican government presupposed a virtuous, and especially God-fearing, citizenry. *Now*, it is carnival in private and conformity in public.

Where should Americans go from here? Catholic teaching is a good place to start.

I

The founders' legacy harmonizes with Catholic teaching. For nearly a century after the founding Church officials abroad (including the Roman Pontiffs) expressed strong reservations about the "separation of church and state." Although the distinction is as old as Jesus's parable about Caesar's coin, its basic meaning in the Catholic tradition retained a commitment to a *Catholic* confessional state wherever possible. (That subject is explored further in the next chapter.) By the pontificate of Leo XIII, however, magisterial teaching was much more forgiving of American-style disestablishment. Leo wrote expressly more than once that the American situation, though not "ideal," could surely be tolerated. There is no doubt whatsoever that there has scarcely been a bishop at *any* point in American history who did not believe that the First Amendment was the best situation for the Church in America. Many prelates spoke rhapsodically about the First Amendment, in both private and public settings. Their true sentiments about the First Amendment were unsparingly positive.

At least since Vatican II, Popes taught that religious liberty is the linchpin or indispensable font of civil liberties and of a flourishing society. As Pope Benedict said in his meeting with the representatives of French culture in 2008: "A purely positivistic culture which tried to drive the question concerning God into the subjective realm, as being unscientific, would be the capitulation of reason, the renunciation of its highest possibilities, and hence a disaster for humanity, with very grave consequences. What gave

Europe's culture its foundation – the search for God, the readiness to listen to him – remains today the basis of any genuine culture." In his 2011 World Day of Peace Message ("Religious Freedom, the Path to Peace") Pope Benedict delivered the most important remarks on the nature and importance of religious freedom of his papacy. He located religious freedom at the base of "all fundamental rights and freedoms, since it is their synthesis and keystone." It is, he said, quoting John Paul II, "the litmus test for the respect of all the other human rights." Benedict added that respect for religious freedom (along with the right to life) "is a condition for the moral legitimacy of every social and legal norm."

II

The lodestar of how Catholics understand religious freedom is the Second Vatican Council's "Declaration" on the subject, *Dignitatis humanae* [DH]. DH says that religious liberty is "immunity from coercion in matters religious." [4]. Because coercion is characteristic of public authority; because of the history and the doctrinal tradition out of which DH consciously emerges; and because much of the first part of DH concerns legitimate limitations upon religious liberty in light of the common good for which public authority bears unique responsibilities, it is understandable to think of religious freedom as strictly a *civil* right. It is correct to think of DH as having much to say about the moral constraints upon the exercise of government's power.

It is also incomplete and misleading to speak in these ways about DH. The liberty affirmed in DH is *not* only a *civil* right. It is a natural right. It is a natural right defined to include a duty of non-interference incumbent not only upon all public authorities, but upon everyone. This "freedom means that all men are to be immune from coercion on the part of *any* human individuals or of social groups and of *any* human power." [2; emphasis added]. "Everyone ought at all times refrain from any manner of action which might seem to carry a hint of coercion or of a kind of persuasion that would be dishonorable or unworthy." [4].

Here is the beating heart religious liberty: respect by *everyone* of *everyone's* freedom of religion. There is an important role for law in protecting persons against the intimidation and manipulation of other people concerning matters religious. But the moral duty to respect religious free-dom falls upon everyone. It seems then to be "all-in" for *freedom* of religion. And that "freedom" consists of what surely appears to be a stridently *neg-ative* liberty: freedom *from*.

Not quite.

Unless this superstructure of mutual restraint and forbearance is suf-fused with the right cultural stuff – inhabited by the proper infrastructure – a scheme overridingly committed to each one's free quest for religious truth is likely to derail into an enabler of individual self-invention, indi-viduality for its own sake, subjectivity or identity. This is approximately the situation in America. This subjectivity is acidic. It corrodes the under-carriage of genuine religious liberty, especially the notion that religion is *about* objective truth. This infrastructure is cultural before it is legal. And without a sound culture of religion surrounding it, it is only a matter of time before the law of religious liberty degenerates into a hallowed subdi-vision of the Mystery Passage.

DH says nothing explicitly about the shape and content of the cultural supports which religious liberty requires for its successful operation in so-ciety. In fact, DH uses the *word* "culture" just twice. The only two uses of the term are the adjectival usage near the end of section 4 ("the right of men freely …to establish educational, *cultural,* charitable and social organ-izations") and in the penultimate paragraph of the document, which refers in a desultory way to men of "different cultures and religion…being brought together." One might even compare this invisibility of culture to the overflowing roster of serious engagements with "culture" in GS, prom-ulgated the same day as DH.

III

We can fill in the missing elements of DH by resort to plain implication and sound inference. Our way is made easier by some reflections of our two recent scholar Popes. Three distinctive relevant emphases are present in their messages. Each emphasis is sound and valuable. Each is truly new. You will find none of them in either DH or in any other Vatican II docu-ment. They are not present in the social encyclicals or anywhere else in the writings of John XXIII or Paul VI. They are not part of the broader tradition of Catholic social teaching stretching back to *Rerum novarum*, Pope Leo XIII's exploration of the "new things" that emerged with the advent of the industrial economy. Indeed, these three papal emphases are only *possible* in the wake of DH.

Pope Saint John Paul II and Pope Emeritus Benedict stressed, *first*, that culture is fundamentally the religious question writ large. Pope John Paul II wrote in his encyclical letter *Centesimus annus* [24]: "At the heart of every culture lies the attitude man takes to the greatest mystery: the mystery of God. Different cultures are basically different ways of facing the question of the meaning of personal existence." As that Pope once said to Francis Cardinal George: "Faith creates culture." Pope Benedict XVI told visiting American bishops in 2012: "At the heart of every culture, whether perceived or not, is a consensus about the nature of reality," which in context meant much of what he meant by "religion." In his 2011 World Day of Peace Message ("Religious Freedom, the Path to Peace") Pope Benedict spoke more pointedly about culture and religious freedom than at any other time. He spoke of "the religious dimension of culture, built up over the centuries thanks to the social and especially ethical contributions of religion." "More important still is religion's ethical contribution in the political sphere." And in his September 12, 2008, speech in Paris, Pope Benedict said: "Religious freedom is…an achievement of a sound political and juridical culture."

Second: *religious liberty is a cultural achievement.* It is not something which is the fruit of the earth or which is so obviously conducive to human happiness that no society could fail to promote it. Religious liberty is a cultural achievement that history and current events show to be uncommon and fragile.

What does that culture look like?

DH describes religious freedom as comprised of two duties. The first binds everyone to refrain from coercion and all manner of unworthy persuasion of others when it comes to religious things. This is *freedom from*. The second is the duty of everyone with regard to religion. It is the correlative *freedom for* each person to carry out his "duty to seek the truth in religious matters."

Essential to the possibility of genuine religious liberty on the ground is a supportive culture characterized by a high degree of commitment to the proposition that religion is a *zone of truth*, and not an enclave of tradition, custom, identity, projections, emotions, and edifying fables. The second is that there is an important, inalienable moral duty to seek out and to embrace religious truth. The third is that religious liberty has to be distinguished from other sorts of liberty, even from the right of conscience. Without these three cultural anchors – and no matter how much freedom from external interference characterizes a society – there simply will not be *religious liberty.*

By "zone of truth" I do not mean that specifically Catholic faith includes assent to true propositions (as we find in the Creed, in the Decalogue, and elsewhere in Scripture where the sacred authors assert a proposition). The foundational part of DH does not depend upon *this* "zone of truth." It depends instead upon an essential precondition, or implication of this "zone": that religion is the kind of thing that is either true or false. "True or false" here means objectively the case, or not. It is not the watered-down subjective sense of "true," such that my religion is "true" for me because it corresponds to my experiences and feelings and expresses them more or less adequately, and your religion is "true" for you, for the same reasons. It is not the more anticipatory truth of self-assertion, or what is often denoted by the term "personal identity," such that one *projects* an idealized image of oneself, and thereafter strives to somehow become that ideal. It is the more common-sense everyday meaning of "true" that the founders surely predicated of religion, and of religious liberty. So should we.

Here it is perhaps most urgent to retrieve and promote some of Pope Benedict's searing comments to Latin American bishops assembled in Aparecida, Brazil, in 2007. He told his listeners, many of whom were still in thrall to liberation theology, that all such political ideologies "falsify the notion of reality by detaching it from the foundational and decisive reality which is God." He explained that "only those who recognize God know reality," and that one "who excludes God from his horizons falsifies the notion of 'reality' and, in consequence, can only end up in blind alleys or with recipes for destruction."

Religion is about reality. The different world religions are and should be apprehended as (in great part) different accounts of that reality, including most especially those spiritual parts which are impervious to measurement and touch, and those realities which can only be known to humankind by God's self-disclosure. Religion is thus answerable to the truth about the universe, all that there is, seen and unseen. Our understanding of all this, though forever incomplete so long as we live on earth, must nonetheless be coherent as far as it goes. So, religion answers to both what is really the case, and to the demands of logic.

Any society's culture and law include manifold and innumerable opportunities to register its understanding of religion as including objective truths about reality. It is most important, however, that the churches (and religious groups and leaders more generally) witness to this way of conceiving the truth about religion. For if they do not, who will?

IV

Everyone's moral responsibility to seek religious truth and to live in accord with it is perhaps the heart of DH. "All men are bound to seek the truth, especially in what concerns God and His Church, and to embrace the truth they come to know, and to hold fast to it." [DH 1]. "All men are impelled by nature and also by moral obligation to seek the truth, especially religious truth. They are also bound to adhere to the truth once it is known, and to order their whole lives in accord with the demands of truth." [DH 2].

Why should this particular moral requirement be so urgent? On what grounds could the recent Popes stress that this question should be the heart of our culture, including our political and legal cultures?

The answer was supplied by a Polish Archbishop when he intervened in the Second Vatican Council's discussion of DH. Speaking on behalf of the entire Polish bishops' conference, Karol Wojtyla asserted that the liberty protected was so large because the corresponding moral duty was so large and pressing. Wojtyla maintained that a person's relationship to God is of "maximal" and everlasting importance. He implied that if this duty should lose its priority in the moral life, then so too will religious liberty lose its pre-eminence in social life.

Getting people to take seriously this moral duty is heavy-going in modern culture. It is not a norm of justice, as if we owe it to other people to seek the truth, and somehow have wronged them if we do not. It is not quite a duty to God; even if it were, modern societies do not much care about such matters. It is not quite a duty to oneself either; even if it were, ignoring it would be what we call now a "victimless immorality," which means for most today: not immoral at all. In any event there is no basis for legally punishing anyone for failing to conscientiously investigate divine matters. And trying to force anyone by less drastic means to perform this moral duty is self-defeating. One person cannot *make* another person honestly believe in the truth of any proposition. Trying to do can only result (at most) in feigned or half-hearted assent.

The only possibly fruitful social input here must be a set of cultural expectations and a whole social milieu in which everyone who values the esteem of others, and who wishes to be involved with his culture's most urgent subject, will naturally want to engage the theological conversation.

The *third* essential part of the infrastructure (recall that the first was that culture is the religious question writ large, and the second is that religious liberty is a cultural achievement), is that *religious liberty has to be distinguished from other sorts of liberties, including liberty of conscience.* Call this the un-Mystery Passage, because it absorbs religious freedom into an undifferentiated right of self-invention. In cultures which were once determined by Christianity, when religion becomes devolved into a non-cognitive enterprise, "religious liberty" can scarcely avoid collapsing into a freedom to manifest one's personal spiritual identity.

V

To detach religious liberty from truth is to decapitate it!

This is unfortunately the danger today in post-Christian societies. The peril is often abetted by treating "religious liberty" as a synonym for "rights of conscience." This conflation is midwifed by the radical subjectivization of religious belief itself. As we saw in Chapter One, vocabularies of self-definition and self-fulfillment stalk today's believers. We saw that conception of religion already prevails in our law, in the academy, and in much of popular religion on the airwaves. It has found its way into even the more traditional churches. The cultural critic Philip Rieff wrote in 2005 "that the orthodox are in the miserable situation of being orthodox for therapeutic reasons." It is the main reason why the non-church of those who are "spiritual" but "not religious" is the fastest growing denomination in America. Each one's experience is the measure of his or her religion, not the other way around. Christians at least used to hold that Jesus was the norm of all our religious experience, including our experience of Him.

In his 2010 Christmas greeting to the Roman Curia Pope Benedict XVI noted that "[i]n modern thinking, the word 'conscience' signifies that for moral and religious questions, it is the subjective dimension, the individual, that constitutes the final authority for decision." So far considered, the Pope's statement could, possibly, be understood in a way compatible with DH. But he observed further that the modern world is "divided into the realms of the objective and the subjective." Religion and morals, the Pope continued, "lie within the subjective realm. Here, it is said, there are in the final analysis no objective criteria. The ultimate instance that can decide here is therefore the subject alone," guided by and indeed governed by his "intuitions and experiences," and not, one might emphasize, objective indicia of truth.

Pope Benedict concluded this portion of his remarks by stating that "conscience is both capacity for truth and obedience to the truth which manifests itself to anyone who seeks it with an open heart." The path of "conversion is a path of conscience – not a path of self-asserting subjectivity but, on the contrary, a path of obedience to truth."

This epochal decline of religious liberty has distant origins in mid-nineteenth century liberal Protestantism, a "religion of the heart" suffused with piety and emotion but in which dogma and doctrine and even revelation as such had no real-world referent. Creeds were not retained as propositional truths about what is. They rather became so many verbal formulae which identified one's particular community of believers. These expressions of community solidarity were not so much true – or false, for that matter. They were no longer the kinds of things that could be either true or false. Already by 1875 Blessed Cardinal Newman (in his Letter to the Duke of Norfolk) wrote: "When men advocate the rights of conscience, they in no sense mean the rights of the creator, nor the duty to Him, in thought and deed, of the creature, but the right of thinking, speaking, writing, and acting, according to their judgment or their humour, without any thought of God at all."

"Modernism" was roughly the counterpart movement within the Catholic Church. Although it was condemned by Pius X in the encyclical *Pascendi Dominici gregis*, in 1907, modernism survived in the Church and flourishes, albeit without being described by either its enthusiasts or its opponents *as* "Modernism." It is a kind of fideism, characterized by a rejection of the possibility that reason and evidence could be sufficient to show that there is a God, that God has communicated reliably to humankind especially by and through His Son, and that the Catholic Church is the vehicle by which that revelation is to be protected, developed, and promulgated. So described by Pope Pius in *Pascendi,* the upshot of this diffidence about reason was that the "evidence" for the truth of religious tenets is supplied by sentiment or experience or some other sort of psychological data.

VI

The present state of affairs in our political culture is rooted most proximately in mid-twentieth century existentialism, when even the staid lawyers on the Supreme Court began seriously elaborating the meaning of our religion clauses, and – before you know it – they were quoting the Protestant existentialist theologian, Paul Tilich!

A most telling illustration of the difference that existentialism makes to religious liberty once it infiltrates a culture's understanding of religion has to do with the former Lord Chancellor of England. More exactly, consider the difference between the playwright Robert Bolt's *Man for All Seasons* and Thomas More, the man who was martyred for his faith and who became a saint.

Thomas More lived in the sixteenth century, long before Modernism intruded upon Catholic convictions. Bolt's play, however, was published in 1960. First produced on Broadway a year later, the Oscar-winning movie came out in 1966. Both productions starred Paul Schofield in the title role.

Bolt wrote – accurately – in his Preface to *A Man for All Seasons* that "on any day up to that of his execution" More could have gone on living if he had been willing to give public approval to Henry's marriage to Anne." He never did. What did he die for? Do you really think it was for a stubborn sense of personal "identity"?

Just after he tells the Duke Norfolk that the English nobility "would have snored through the Sermon on the Mount," Bolt's More exclaims: "And what would you do with a water spaniel that was afraid of water? You'd hang it! Well, as a spaniel is to water, so is a man to his own self. I will not give in because I oppose – I do – not my pride, not my spleen, not any other of my appetites but I do – I!" The added emphases correspond to Schofield's in the film, and surely in the stage production as well.

In the Preface to the play Bolt confessed that "Thomas More became for me a man with an adamantine sense of his own self." Bolt apologized – his word – for treating Thomas More, a Christian saint, "as a hero of selfhood."

Robert Bolt's own convictions shine through in his lament: "It may be that a clear sense of the self can only crystallize around something transcendental, in which case, our prospects look poor, for we are rightly committed to the rational." Our most gifted men, on the other hand, should labor "to get a sense of selfhood without resort to magic. Albert Camus is a writer I admire in this connection." It is as if Bolt subscribed to the Mystery Passage.

Bolt's existential More is not Thomas More, any more than Albert Camus is a Christian saint. For More, for any saint, for any martyr is nothing but a fool without the Truth. After all, the Greek root of "martyr" is simply "witness." And that means witness to Truth.

After speaking of John Henry Newman in a 1991 lecture, then Cardinal Ratzinger turned to the one whom he called "Britain's other great witness of conscience, Thomas More, for whom conscience was not at all an expression of subjective stubbornness or obstinate heroism." Ratzinger said that "conscience is both capacity for truth and obedience to the truth which manifests itself to anyone who seeks it with an open heart." The path of "conversion is a path of conscience – not a path of self-asserting subjectivity but, on the contrary, a path of obedience to truth."

The point can scarcely be overstressed: once religion and "truth" decompose into the sort of personal "authenticity" and subjectivism described so far, then the *meaning* of "conscience" in the phrase, *it is a tenet of justice that within certain limits everyone's freedom of conscience be respected,* is shifted and attenuated. It is shifted to what we see in Bolt's More – a stubborn and admirable up to a point individuality. Its value is attenuated, too, because the *harm* of violating one's "conscience" so understood is reduced essentially to a very bad feeling, a sense of being violated, of felt constraint upon how one would express oneself.

Conclusion

Religious liberty is in danger of disappearing into the maws of the super-liberty to define, and even to invent, oneself. The American Catholic Church is so crippled by apostasy and moral that it seems fantastical to suppose it could spearhead a revival of fortunes for our "first freedom." Catholics cannot expect their friends in political life to help the Church now – the "optics" of protecting the Church's prerogatives are now bleak. Only the most courageous judges will apply the law evenhandedly now, too, where doing so protects the Church. There is nonetheless no alternative to plunging into the public debate and fearlessly speaking truth to power.

This too has happened before. One time was the time of Thomas More. The scene was described by my colleague John Finnis. More was in the Tower of London, awaiting an interrogation, and "[o]ut of the windows of another room in the Palace, looking into the garden below, More could see – as doubtless he was meant to see – the clergy of London passing through the garden." As Finnis depicts the scene: "Most of them were cheerful enough, slapping each other on the back and calling for beer at the Archbishops' buttery. All took the oath, save one who was hurried through the garden on his way to the Tower, where he would languish for three years until he accepted the Protestant order."

Those back-slappers in cassocks lived on, for a little while. Most of them no doubt died in their beds, perhaps heedless until the end of Saint James epistolary admonition: "Come now, you who say, 'today or tomorrow we shall go to such and such a town, spend a year there, and come off with a profit?' You have no idea what kind of life will be yours tomorrow. You are a vapor that appears briefly and vanishes." [James 4:13-15]

Who were these men ambling towards the archbishop's "buttery"? What were their names? No one remembers. They are all long forgotten. But Saint Thomas More and Saint John Fisher are not. They are an inspiration to every steward of the truth, then, now, and until the end of the age.

Chapter 3
The American State and Religious Truth

In the memory of many still living it was customary for Americans to affirm the transcendent bases of human dignity and equality. Many still do. In the Declaration of Independence our founders declared: "We hold these truths to be self-evident, that all men are created equal, that they are endowed by their Creator with certain unalienable rights, that among these are life, liberty, and the pursuit of happiness." In 1963 (in the case of *School District of Abington Township v. Schempp,* which pertained to Bible-reading in public schools) the Supreme Court said that the "fact that the Founding Fathers believed devotedly that there was a God and the inalienable rights of man were rooted in Him is clearly evidenced in their writings, from the Mayflower Compact to the Constitution itself."

Every day most Americans implicitly join this chorus, for anyone who handles a dollar bill carries our national Motto: "In God we Trust." Those who attend sporting events or who watch one on television might hear a rendition of "God Bless America." Any civic occasion with a historical element is likely to include reference to a forefather who spoke devotedly – as Lincoln perhaps most famously did at Gettysburg or in his justly famous Second Inaugural – of a righteous and providential God who superintends human affairs. Legislators from the United States Congress down to the humblest county school board regularly open their deliberations with prayer, a hallowed practice that the Supreme Court has consistently and as recently as 2014 (in the case of *Greece v. Galloway)* upheld as constitutional. The Justices would have heard those cases after the Marshall heralded their sitting, declaring "God Save this Honorable Court."

All these – and many other – public acknowledgements and professions of religious belief fit uneasily into the prevailing jurisprudence of church and state. They do not fit at all with the prevailing cultural convictions expressed centrally by the Mystery Passage. The courts struggle mightily with the jurisprudential issues, because although these holy exercises *are* inconsistent with modern doctrine of the First Amendment, they are wholly continuous with unbroken historical practices that started with the founders. Contemporary elites do not struggle with but rather unrepentantly oppose all these practices, and work to overthrow them.

The First Amendment Establishment Clause is the primary relevant text. It says that "Congress [and by extension all government entities] shall make no law respecting an establishment of religion." An "establishment" referred at the founding to the sort of confessional state exemplified by Anglican England. We shall investigate the question of religious truth and the state in America in this chapter by, first, examining two relevant questions (more or less running together, through several sections of the chapter) about a Catholic "establishment": whether such a "confessional" state is permissible when measured by the authoritative teaching of *Dignitatis humane* ("*DH*"), and whether it is simply unjust. The answers are, I shall contend, that a Catholic "confessional" state is permissible under *DH* and is not unjust.

Then we shall turn to a more thorough consideration of the American constitutional settlement. Although it is surely true that a Catholic "establishment" would violate the First Amendment, the tradition is much more friendly to religion, and even to an implicit establishment of Christianity, than contemporary church-state jurisprudence and its cultural correspondents indicate. Finally, we shall consider the arguments of "integralists," who maintain that a Catholic "confessional" state is today not only permissible but necessary. Integralists such as Thomas Pink and Edward Waldstein, O. Cist., often argue that Church teaching up to and including *DH requires* a Catholic establishment where feasible. In this chapter I leave aside this precise question about Church teaching and logical necessity. I look instead at the integralists' more inductive argument that a Catholic confessional state is practically necessary, that the real common good can hardly be maintained without one.

I

What an achievement *Dignitatis humanae* was! In the more than fifty years since it was promulgated near the end of the Second Vatican Council, nothing of an authoritative nature has been added to its main propositions. None has been the subject of authoritative modification or clarification. Pope Benedict XVI spoke very forcefully about a "healthy secularism" (especially in France, in 2008), and in defense of a stout conception of religious liberty (most prominently to visiting American bishops in early 2012). In none of these talks, however, did the Pope suggest that *DH* needed revision or updating. On the contrary: in many diverse venues, both John Paul II and Benedict XVI robustly defended the Council's teaching about religious liberty as not only an important human right, but as a bulwark of other rights and as the linchpin of the free society.

Dignitatis humanae is now nested within a broad secular consensus about religious liberty, a consensus which includes foundational international legal documents. The precise manner of reconciling the teaching of *DH* with the tradition of Catholic thought which preceded it is debated by a small number of exceptionally able scholars. These matters are not the concern here. In the first part of this chapter I take up one question, however, about what *DH means*. Is the teaching of *DH* compatible with state recognition of Catholicism as the true religion?

II

John Courtney Murray, S.J., was America's leading Catholic public intellectual between World War II and Vatican II; at least if Fulton Sheen is to be considered an apologist and not a "public intellectual." During those years Murray defended the patriotism of Catholics and the Church's fit with American democracy against Protestants (and others) skeptical of both. Murray chided Protestants, too, for their myopia. The real threat to them was not the Catholic Church, he argued presciently, but the rapidly emerging secularism which would privatize and thereby impoverish all religions in America. Murray's criticisms of the Court's "wall of separation" between church and state (which he knew was informed by latent anti-Catholicism) were often spot-on. He was especially keen to deny Protestants' claims to own the First Amendment by virtue of supplying the intellectual categories necessary to understand and apply it. The Religion Clauses were not, Murray famously argued, "Articles of Faith." They were instead "Articles of Peace," good positive laws which carried modest anthropological and moral baggage.

Though Murray's distinction between "articles" could not bear all the weight he put on it, he was right to say – as he repeatedly insisted – that the Religion Clauses do *not* forbid government aid to religion so long as no discrimination among religions is made. This "non-preferentialism" remains the standing alternative to the no-aid-at-all to religion rule which the Court imported into the First Amendment, starting in the 1947 *Everson* case, and which it has foisted upon America since. Murray left no doubt, either, that if the Supreme Court moved to privatize religion, the whole American Catholic community would dissent. On this he was not so prescient. The Court has indeed privatized religion (about as much as it is institutionally able to do). America's Catholics have not risen in dissent as a body.

Some Catholic intellectuals have gone beyond just praise of Murray as a public intellectual. Historians Scott Appleby and John Haas, for example, say that "Murray's interpretation of church and state would carry the day at the Second Vatican Council." I disagree. It is true that Murray's conclusion about the civil liberty of non-Catholics to publicly profess and practice their faiths *is* found in *DH*. Non-Catholics (the Council Fathers taught) do indeed have a right to immunity from coercion when they do so. But Murray's supporting arguments differed from those of the Fathers. His central argument against repressing heresy was also the central aim of all his church-state reflections: the state – in some necessary or universal sense – is *incompetent* to recognize the true religion. This guiding conviction implies, of course, that no state may recognize Catholicism as true.

Is this the teaching of *DH*?

The question is a live one. The Council Fathers left "untouched" the "traditional Catholic doctrine on the moral duty of men and societies toward the true religion and toward the one Church of Christ" (*DH* 1). But they did not say what the "teaching" was. In the years since 1965, the Church has scarcely clarified the matter; the whole question of state recognition of the true faith has been neglected. Neither Pope John Paul II nor Benedict XVI has spoken a favorable word for any kind of Catholic "establishment." The *Catechism* affirms that "[t]he duty of offering God genuine worship concerns man both individually and socially," but it does not say much more about it. Further exploration of *DH*'s teaching is therefore in order.

III

In the following pages I shall state and then refute three arguments for the view that it is unconditionally *wrong* – unjust – for the state to recognize the Catholic Church as the true church, even where political circumstances, such as an overwhelmingly Catholic population in a democratic polity, would permit it. After stating each argument I try to show it is unsound as an interpretation of *DH and* as a matter of unrestricted moral reasoning.

My exploration of the state's competence on religion is aided and illustrated by frequent reference to Murray's post-World War II exchanges with three fellow American priests – Monsignor Joseph Fenton, Rev. Francis Connell, C.S.S.R., and Rev. George Shea – on the subject of religious liberty. Of these interlocutors Appleby and Haas report that "Fenton and Connell, by contrast [to Murray], would be relegated to the dubious status of also-rans, the import of their own theological work reduced almost in direct proportion to the gathering prominence of Murray's." This judgment is shared by most Catholic intellectuals.

The judgment is undeserved. There is much to criticize in the three traditionalists' reasoning. Their position on the liceity of repressing heresy was, moreover, rightly rejected by the Council. But the Council adhered to the "traditional" teaching about the state's competence to recognize the true Church. The three priests' arguments (especially those of Connell) were equal to Murray's in clarity and cogency.

Murray's most complete response to Connell (a reply to Connell's "The Theory of the Lay State") was a disaster. By that time, Murray's impatience with his opponents had ripened into condescension. He bullied Connell and butchered Connell's arguments, accusing him of (among other sins) "logicism," which Murray defined as "the achievement of a pseudoconsequence by a concatenation of propositions that represent mere conceptualizations." Connell drily observed that this was "a somewhat complicated way of saying that I am rather stupid." Murray was often that pompous, and condescending.

Francis Connell was surely no idiot. His fear was that once Catholics were assimilated into middle-class American culture they would be prone to *indifferentism*. Connell seems to have been right about this. In fact, a reexamination of this whole exchange – without prejudice by the intellectuals' verdict for Murray – may refresh our understanding of what the Church authoritatively teaches about religious liberty, the state, and the true faith.

Is it necessarily wrong for the state to recognize Catholicism as true? Would it be wrong if, in the Preamble of a Constitution, the people (presumably, of an overwhelmingly Catholic polity) said something like: "We hereby profess and declare that our religion – the Catholic religion – is true and that the fullness of truth subsists only in the Catholic Church."

The question is *not* about the legitimacy or wisdom of the First Amendment, which surely does prohibit recognition of Catholicism – or any other faith – as true. As a matter of historical fact, American Catholics who have objected to the First Amendment as unjust or immoral – or even as bad for the Catholic Church – have been very few. The Third Plenary Council of the American Bishops (1884) said: "We consider the establishment of our country's independence, the shaping of its liberties, as a work of Providence, its framers 'building better than they knew,' the Almighty's hand guiding them." Father Connell said, too, that "Catholics have no intention or desire of modifying the system prevailing under our Constitution, the system of allowing all our citizens full liberty of conscience, complete equality of all religious denominations before the law." Connell later said that the American prohibition on showing special favor to any particular religion "is perfectly reasonable and in no way opposed to the law of Christ."

IV

The three arguments *against* this sort of legal action that I shall examine are:

1. Recognition of the true faith would be an "act of faith," and the state is incapable of an "act of faith" (a first "incompetence" argument).

2. Recognition would require the state to act on the basis of information or belief which is revealed and not available to unaided reason. But the state would exceed its competence (its just bounds) if it acted on the basis of revelation (a second "incompetence" argument).

3. Recognition would exceed the bounds of the political common good, the justifying principle and outer limit of the state's authority (a third "incompetence" argument).

A. In response to Argument 1: Metaphysical Incompetence

"[I]n what sense can the state, as a set of institutions, a function, an agency, make an act of divine faith or profess a religion?" Murray posed this question in response to Father Shea's description of the state as a "creature of God." Murray said that Shea's choice of words made "plausible" the notion that the "state" – this "creature of God" – could make an "act of faith." Murray replied that the state just is not that kind of thing.

In his paper "Catholic Doctrine and 'The Religion of the State,'" Shea had indeed made an unfortunate argument about the state's duty to worship God by virtue of its membership in a class – "creatures of God" – to which men and women also belonged. This expression was at least incautious. Murray was right to stress the "fictive" quality of saying that the state was a "person." But Murray was ungenerous in ascribing to Shea an "hypostatized concept of the state." For by "creature of God" Shea did not mean that the "state" possessed consciousness and free will and a soul, as do persons. He clearly meant that the state was part of God's plan, and that government is morally legitimate and even necessary to mankind's well-being – and that the state was under a moral duty regarding religious truth similar to the duty of persons. Shea was saying, basically, that the state was part of God's providential plan for humankind.

So it is. As Father Connell said plainly in one of his early interventions, the "parallel between personal and civic duties" toward the law of Christ (of which Pius XI spoke in *Quas primas*) "cannot be followed out in every respect. A government cannot be baptized, nor is it liable to eternal damnation." And, for what it is worth, contemporary "integralists" such as Thomas Pink do not suggest that the state can, or should attempt to, make "acts of faith" so far described here.

It is true the state cannot make *certain* acts of faith. But it can perform the act (and mental operations) necessary to affirm that Catholicism is true. The state *is* capable of affirming propositions. It does affirm propositions all the time. Apart from countless propositions about what is the case which laws *imply*, lawmaking authorities often affirm the truth about disputed matters, just to say it. It is much easier to see the sense of Shea's assertions if we substitute the word "lawmakers" for "state" in his declarative sentences. Sometimes in statutes and sometimes in constitutions, whether as "findings" or as a Preamble or merely precatory language, public authorities assert this or that proposition. There is nothing unusual about a legislative declaration that, for example, a human individual comes to be at conception, or about a whole national body politic declaring, for example, that "a well regulated militia [is] necessary to the security of a free state," as "we, the people" of the United States affirmed in the Second Amendment.

It is true that such declarations usually are followed by an operative directive (". . . and everyone shall at stated times come and perform their duty of . . ."). Legislative bodies, executive officers, courts, and grand juries often enough issue proclamations, resolutions, reports and presentments simply, and solely, declaring what is the case. There is nothing mysterious or untoward in saying that the "state declares" (or even that the "mind of the lawmaker is . . .") where the acts and utterances of a collective body are at issue, any more than it is mysterious to speak that way of, say, the Second Vatican Council, whose documents speak the mind of the "Council," even where there were dissenting voices.

There is a substantial difference, to put it another way, between *recognizing* the truth of any set of propositions – including propositions about God – and *professing* faith or *making an act of* faith. The latter undertakings include more than recognition of certain truths. They include adhesion to and trust in the object of faith, acts which the state can scarcely be imagined to make. So far considered there is no reason to doubt that the state is *able* to do what it takes to recognize – affirm, declare – that Catholicism is true.

B. In response to Argument 2: Epistemic Incompetence

Murray maintained that the state should act only on the basis of unaided human reason. "As the law for man emerges from the nature of man as elevated by grace, so the law for the state emerges from the nature of the state, which was not elevated by grace." Murray consistently emphasized throughout his writings that the state's "competence" did not extend to matters of revelation or to the "supernatural" realm. He clearly held, too, that one implication or entailment of this position was that the true religion could not be identified by the state.

According to Connell, Murray here took over and supported the views of John of Paris, who famously maintained (according to Connell) that the limits of the prince's "direct power" are set by "natural law." In reply to

Murray (and John), Connell subtly evaded the effect of Murray's way of stating the question. For Murray the division was between "nature" and "reason" on one side, and "grace" and "revelation" on the other. Connell pointed out, however, that the "*temporal* is not identical with the *natural*." Connell then said that it could be the case – that indeed it *was* the case – that certain matters which fell under the "natural law" jurisdiction of the state were also under the Church's jurisdiction. "[I]f Jesus Christ has actually granted the Church authority over certain matters which civil rulers would possess by virtue of the natural law, it follows that civil rulers have a correlative obligation to obey the divine positive law in respect to these matters." Connell cited as examples the law of marriage impediments and the dissolution of certain valid marriages (the Pauline privilege).

I am not sure that Connell was right to say that the state should involve itself in marriage norms so far as to recognize the Pauline privilege. But he was right about two larger points, and these are enough to rebut Murray's argument. Connell's first point was that, insofar as a lawmaker believes that his duties require him to decide some matter, and insofar as he believes that some necessary premise of deciding what he is charged to decide can only be known by revelation, the lawmaker must decide the matter by relying upon revelation. For example: if a lawmaker believes that one can only know the *truth* of when people begin by virtue of Scripture (the baby leapt in Elizabeth's womb), or because of some theological proposition taught by the Church (the soul is infused at conception), then the lawmaker is obliged to act on that *truth,* wherever he or she has found it. If justice requires that the lawmaker resort to knowledge unavailable to reason alone, then it cannot be unjust for the lawmaker to go beyond natural law.

I think that Connell is right about this.

Connell's second point was that, whether lawmakers may or must go beyond unaided reason in the discharge of their tasks does not affect the question of state recognition of Catholicism as true. In one "Reply to Father Murray" Connell correctly identified what he called a "vital defect" in this part of Murray's thought: "he [Murray] does not distinguish between the preamble of faith, the motives of credibility and the judgment of credibility . . . on the one hand, and the truths of faith, the motive of faith, and the act of faith on the other hand." The former are "natural," he said, and the latter are "supernatural." To recognize Catholicism as true does *not* require resort to revelation (though, of course, once one recognizes Catholicism as true, one will credit a number of revealed truths).

Connell was right about this, too.

C. In response to Argument 3: Moral Incompetence

DH avoids all expressions which smack of mystification or "hypostatization" of the state. Nothing in that document's description of the state likens it to "God's creatures." One main concern of the document is to mark an all-important *limit* upon the state's jurisdiction. *DH*'s larger account of political society and its distinctive common good shows it to be subsidiary, instrumental, limited to the important but circumscribed role of *assisting* persons to achieve *their* perfection. The state, as the administrative arm of the political society, works within the limited scope of the political common good.

DH also affirms the truth that "religious acts" – at least those "whereby men, in private and in public and out of a sense of personal conviction, direct their lives to God" – transcend "the order of terrestrial and temporal affairs." It is obviously true that neither the state nor any other external observer can unfailingly read what is in another's heart. The state is mainly concerned with regulating external behavior.

Is it the teaching of *DH* that state affirmation of Catholicism's truth is wrong because – even if the state can recognize Catholicism as true – the truth of the matter is beyond the just bounds of political society's scope? Even if it could, it should not?

No. In *DH* the Council Fathers affirmed what they describe as "traditional Catholic doctrine." Father Brian Harrison has argued persuasively and on abundant evidence that the "traditional" teaching was that the "civic community as such has a duty to honor God, and to recognize as uniquely true the religion entrusted by Christ to the Catholic Church." (See his excellent book, *Religious Liberty and Contraception,* a masterly treatment of Church teaching.)

In section 13 of *DH* the Fathers declared that the "freedom of the Church is the fundamental principle in what concerns the relations between the Church and governments and the whole civil order." "As the spiritual authority appointed by Christ the Lord with the duty, imposed by divine command, of going into the whole world and preaching the Gospel to every creature, the church claims freedom for itself in human society and before every public authority."

In *DH* the Fathers advance two grounds for this judgment. One has to do with the Church's "character as a society of men who have the right to live in society in accordance with the precepts of the Christian faith," as would (I suppose) other such "societies." The other ground is this: "In human society and in the face of government the Church claims freedom for herself in her character as a spiritual authority established by Christ the Lord, upon which there rests, by divine mandate, the duty of going out into the whole world and preaching the Gospel to every creature."

This freedom is described just above in the text of *DH* as the "full measure of freedom," the "sacred freedom," "sacred" because purchased by Christ with His blood. To the concern expressed by several influential Fathers that (in Father Harrison's account of it) "the Declaration should 'set out the particular right of the Church to diffuse truth – a right which she alone possesses,'" Bishop De Smedt (the *relator)* said that it was already sufficiently covered in the text. I think that *DH* 13 calls for the state to consider the Church's claim to be true and implies that the state would act justly by accepting that claim.

In the most relevant respects, Father Connell anticipated *DH* 13 and stated its substance as an argument against Murray. Fr. Connell made his proto-*DH* argument in his "Theory of the Lay State," and in a brief "Reply to Father Murray." Murray's response is called "For The Freedom and Transcendence of the Church." This is the paper I earlier described as a "disaster."

Section 6 of *DH* may reinforce this reading of section 13. In *DH* 6 the Council Fathers recognized that "peculiar circumstances" might result in "special civil recognition" of "one religious community in the constitutional order of society." Even here, however, the text refers back to the individual and corporate religious liberty which must in every case be respected. The language of *DH* here is entirely generic. It could stand an interpretation (or contemplates an application) where Islam or Hinduism or some other non-Catholic faith has been established. It seems rather more likely, though, that the Fathers here took the "internal" point of view, and that their attention was directed principally to Catholic populations which have made a special place in their constitutional schemes for the true faith. Even in such cases, the state must respect the rights of non-Catholics to immunity from coercion.

Apart from the authority of *DH*, is recognition of Catholicism as uniquely true beyond the scope of the political common good? I think that, in light of the educative function of the law and the epistemic authority which the state in modern societies possesses, the answer is "no," so long (of course) as the immunity of all persons from coercion in religious matters (within due limits) is respected. Sometimes at least, state recognition of the true faith could be a useful aid to persons' search for religious truth and a valuable guide to lawmakers in their work.

DH teaches what reason itself shows: because men's religious acts "transcend" temporal affairs, government "therefore ought indeed take account of the religious life of the citizenry and show it favor, since the function of government is to make provision for the common welfare." Thus government must understand and act on the understanding that religion is not only free and transcendent, but also earth-bound so that it is possible and necessary for government to promote it, so long as coercion is avoided. "However, it would clearly transgress the limits set to its power, were it to presume to command or inhibit acts that are religious" (*DH* 3).

The state's jurisdiction is wider than its coercive authority. The state engages in non-coercive actions directing persons towards their perfection, steering them away from vice, encouraging them to do what is morally required (but which the state cannot command or prohibit), assisting the non-political institutions of civil society (including the Church) to contribute as it might to the common good and also to the perfection of its members.

The "perfection" of persons lies beyond the ken of political life, even beyond this world entirely. But it does not follow that the "conditions" which contribute to that perfection lie beyond the *eschaton*. They do not. The prudent lawmaker charged with maintaining conditions conducive to persons' achievement of their perfection (in "a certain fullness of measure and also with some relative ease") would benefit by *knowing* contours of that perfection which lies outside this life. The lawmaker *qua* lawmaker may be better off (other things being equal) for knowing the truth about religion.

Murray correctly saw what the Fathers at Vatican II implicitly recognized: saying "error has no rights" does not settle the question about the way the state ought to regard non-Catholics' public religious acts. Persons (and groups) have many rights which do not depend for their existence or for their scope on the right-holder's possession of sound opinions or good character. Married couples have many rights of privacy over and against the state which do not depend upon their performance as spouses. All they need to do to claim these rights is to *be* married. Many very poor works of art and literature enjoy various legal protections just the way Shakespeare does.

The point is that this important civil right attaches to a generic sort of act or status and thus to *all* the members of a class. The right to immunity from coercion of which *DH* speaks attaches to "religious matters" and to all those "acts" whereby anyone tries to learn or abide by the truth about God. The categories "true" or "false" as they pertain to propositions about God have no traction on *this* right, which depends rather for its sound application upon the presence of honest questioning, seeking, adhering, and abiding by the truth.

Murray appears to have thought that the incompetence of the state was an essential premise of any case for the freedom of non-Catholics to publicly profess and practice their faiths. He could not, in other words, escape the grip of "error has no rights." Murray knew that Catholicism was true. But he could not see how, if the state knew it too, "error" could enjoy civil tolerance. Murray therefore grounded an equal right to religious liberty *precisely* on shielding the state from the truth about the Church. To this significant extent, we are very fortunate that Murray's views did *not* "carry the day" at Vatican II.

V

The constitutional settlement which endured for almost two centuries until uprooted in the 1960s was basically this: public authority could and did promote religion and partner with religious institutions for projects conducive to the common good, without coercion and without partiality towards any particular faith or sect. This settlement included the political community's affirmation of certain truths about God. These affirmations did not include sectarian tenets, theological speculation, or assertedly revealed truths. They did include divine realities affirmed in the Declaration of Independence – a unitary God who created all there is, who providentially guides human events, and whose effects included naturally known moral truths, which could be and were known by reason alone.

These truths are elements of a "natural theology" or "natural religion," really a branch of philosophy, and are a reflection on the existence and nature of God using only the power of human reason, operating on data available to everyone. Promoting respect for and belief in them was part of the common good entrusted to the care of public authority.

The founders' pivotal insight was that the truth about sectarian matters – sacred doctrine, modes of worship, forms of church polity, rules for church membership in good standing – could be kept out of political life. Such matters were not unimportant. But arbitrating them need not be the civil magistrate's task. Theologians might contend over the details of faith and worship. But to the statesman they could be matters of opinion.

The First Amendment put the churches on equal legal footing. Full extension or unbiased application of this constitutional norm was not, however, the work of a single generation. The story of how America realized its dream of religious equality is the story of how America weaned itself of a narrow identification of its religious underpinnings with Protestantism, particularly with the "mainline" churches. It is also a story of considerable political conflict and more than occasional injustice toward minority religious groups, most importantly toward Roman Catholics.

The founders' decision to promote and to partner with religion was extraordinary because American religion has never been an aggregate of private spiritualities, so many ineffable experiences of the "inner light." American religion has always been a highly cognitive enterprise, lodged in organized bodies with long histories, dynamic internal imperatives, and audible institutional voices. American' dominant religion, Christianity, has always held that within the one political community are two legitimate authorities, the temporal and the spiritual. The American states' collaboration with free churches has been an often unquiet coexistence between independent forces, each with the resources to take care of itself and to contend with the other free of intimidation or undue deference.

The founders' ingenious settlement has never been entirely abandoned by the American people, with whom it still resonates as fair and good. But the Supreme Court repudiated it, declaring it abandoned in 1947, and then rabidly implementing a secularist imposter Establishment Clause starting with the 1962 public-school prayer case, *Engel v. Vitale*. In that case the Court struck down a pure statement of truths of natural theology in, "Almighty God we acknowledge our dependence upon thee, and we beg Thy blessings upon us, our parents, our teachers, and our Country." No student was obliged to recite the prayer. Nevertheless, *Engel* stuck down recitation of the prayer. Affirming the truths of natural theology was now unconstitutional.

Even though the First Amendment stipulates that the truth or falsity of putatively revealed – that is, beyond the reach of unaided reason – propositions is beyond the scope of political society, those with care for its common good can, and should, recognize the truths of natural religion, including the truth that a divine entity created what there is and sustains it in being (as America's political leaders invariably did, at least until recently). It is reasonable for those charged with such care (as it is reasonable for everybody else) to further expect that such an entity would communicate somehow with humankind. It is thus reasonable to hold – on philosophical grounds – that genuine revelation is not only possible, but likely.

VI

Here is one apt illustration of the founding settlement in action.

On January 21, 1853, the United States Senate Committee on the Judiciary issued its report on "sundry petitions" previously referred to it. These petitions "pray[ed that] Congress abolish the office of Chaplain." The "sundry" petitioners were unidentified. Their claim was nonetheless clear and bold: legal provisions for chaplains in the army and navy as well as in the two houses of Congress violated the First Amendment. To decide upon the correctness of the petitioners' claim, the Committee asked: "what is meant by th[e] expression an establishment of religions"? "[W]ithout doubt," the Senators answered, it referred to "establishment" in the "mother country, and its meaning is to be ascertained by ascertaining what that establishment was." What was the material meaning? "[T]he union of church and state of which our ancestors were so justly jealous." That "connection" or "union with the state of a particular religious society" was characterized "by giving its members exclusive political rights" by "compelling the attendance of those who rejected its communion upon its worship or religious observances," and by giving it all which was withheld from other churches.

In selecting chaplains, Congress took no action liable to objection on establishment grounds so described. "[I]n this, no religion, no form of faith, no denomination of religious preferences, is established, in preference to any other, or has any peculiar privileges conferred up it." Did the Senators here refer to chaplains who sought the lowest common denominational denominator, men who expressed no discernibly sectarian message, who spoke fluent spiritual Esperanto? No. "Selections, in point of fact, are always made from some one of the denominations into which Christians are distributed."

The Committee's statement illustrates an intention to promote the religious life of the people, which happens to be a Christian people, without *quite* affirming their religion to be true:

> This results from the fact that we are a Christian people – from the fact that almost our entire population belong to or sympathise with some one of the Christian denominations which compose the Christian world. And Christians will of course select, for the performance of religious services, one who professes the faith of Christ. This, however, it should be carefully noted, is not by virtue of provision, but voluntary choice. We are Christians, not because the law demands it, not to gain exclusive benefits, or to avoid legal disabilities, but from choice and education; and in a land thus universally Christian, what is to be expected, what desired but that we shall pay a due regard to Christianity, and have a reasonable respect for it ministers and religious solemnities?

The Senators affirmed that where the reason for a law was the spiritual comfort and needs of a body of citizens, it would be the case that their preferences ("voluntary choice") settled the matter rightly: which sort of spiritual comfort? In their penultimate paragraph, however, the antebellum Senators affirmed the constitutional faith of the fathers. They held fast to inherited legal doctrines and to the overarching "natural religion" which they affirmed:

Our fathers were true lovers of liberty, and utterly opposed to any constraint upon the rights of conscience. They intended, by this amendment, to prohibit "an establishment of religion" such as the English church presented, or anything like it. But they had no fear or jealousy of religion itself, nor did they wish to see us an irreligious people; they did not intend to prohibit a just expression of religious devotion by the legislators of the nation, even in their public character as legislators; they did not intend to send our armies and navies forth to do battle for the country without any national recognition of that God on whom success or failure depends; they did not intend to spread over all the public authorities and the whole public action of the nation the dead and revolting spectacle of atheistical apathy. Not so had the battles of the revolution been fought, and the deliberations of the revolutionary Congress conducted. On the contrary, all had been done with a continual appeal to the Supreme Ruler of the world, and an habitual reliance upon His protection of the righteous cause which they commended to His care.

VII

Our constitutional tradition overwhelmingly testifies to the robust faculty of unaided reason, eminently capable of affirming on the basis of evidence and logic a large range of truths about divine matters and about the divine-human relationship. The First Amendment does not stymie the path of this human faculty; on the contrary, its relevant command amounts to a strategic, practical (not moral or epistemological) prohibition upon public authority: none shall make the truth or falsity of a limited number of strictly *theological* matters a basis for action. Without asserting that all of the subjects about which public authority is put under a stipulated agnosticism pertain to revelation, the fact is that most do and it is therefore convenient to describe this bundle as "revealed."

Public authority in America is certainly free to identify and rely upon all the truths of morality and of natural theology which are needed to perform the invaluable work of promoting the common good. There are also good grounds (short of a frank declaration that Christianity is *true*) for treating it almost as if it is. Indeed, it has been the predominate opinion of American lawmakers and probably most citizens that, when pressed to pass judgment, Christianity *is* true. Notwithstanding my own judgment that unaided reason supplies sufficient bases to affirm that the Catholic Church is indeed the true Church – as the Church's traditional apologetic holds – frank affirmation *by the state* of that truth is indeed violative of the First Amendment. Public officials who are Catholic should nonetheless rely upon all the truths they hold which are relevant to their public actions, when performing their duties. Nothing in the Constitution properly interpreted requires otherwise.

This is the context in which to consider the arguments of Catholic integralists in favor of the "confessional state." Their reflections have some of the flavor of thought experiments, for they realize that it is not only far-fetched to speak of a Catholic confessional state today. They know it would be unconstitutional for any state authority to "confess" (and thereby to "establish") Catholicism. Apart from this constitutional prohibition, the practical appetite for such a confession, even among Catholics, is very small. The arguments of "integralists" such as Thomas Pink and Edward Waldstein, O. Cist., are nonetheless worth taking very seriously, for their reflections include spot-on diagnoses of many pathologies affecting our political community, and their prescriptions – short of actually "establishing" Catholicism – are often correct.

I shall take as a conversation partner the best succinct statement of the integralist case I have seen, Pink's "In Defense of Integralism," which was published in *Public Discourse* on August 12, 2018. Pink states plainly: "The state should publicly recognize the truth of the Catholic religion." Pink states that "*Integralism – the need for a confessional Catholic state – is part of Catholic teaching about grace.*" (emphasis added). Here as well as elsewhere in his fine essay, Pink's argument seems to be strictly theological, as if the requirement of a Catholic state could be deduced, or derived as a strong inference, from Scripture or other revealed truths or from authoritative magisterial teachings. I propose to leave aside here what I call with some caution these arguments *from the top down*. The reason is that Pink's arguments *from below* are more relevant to the concerns of this book, are more easily grasped, and because they are so largely sound.

Pink is exactly right when he writes that with "political secularization we find states ... departing from natural law on an ever-widening field of issues, including abortion, euthanasia, and marriage." Moreover, the "secularizing state bears increasingly false witness to the common good. It moves with depressing speed, in many countries, to repress and marginalize opposing Christian witness to the natural law in public life." The argument becomes less certain when Pink turns to *why,* or perhaps better, *how,* a public confession of Catholicism gets the "state" on track. In one articulation of his answer, Pink does not seemingly seek to establish more than what this book contends for, with the caveat that this book does not call for a Catholic "establishment" at all.

Pink writes that

> The reason is that the state's grasp of public reason depends on its public commitment to religious truth. This is owing to the Fall, which has not destroyed human reason, but which has still seriously corrupted it. Divine grace, received with faith and through the sacraments, is needed as *gratia sanans* to restore our damaged rationality. This is true not just in relation to private reason but in relation to public reason too. Baptism obligates Christians, where they can, to commit their political community publicly to Christ.

All that Pink recommends in the preceding paragraph could be accomplished if ordinary citizens, along with those of their number who exercise public authority, put into practice (where appropriate) all the moral and religious truths they hold, a project which clear-headed reasoning requires and to which a Catholic "establishment" is unnecessary. Pink adds that the "state should be Catholic, *or at least broadly Christian,* not because the state is a believer to be saved as an individual is, but because political authority has been divinely established to confess public reason in the service of a genuinely common good." Again: these persuasive concerns could be made operational without a Catholic "confessional" state, as Pink perhaps implicitly recognizes by stating the alternative, "broadly Christian." And America for most of its history has had a "broadly Christian" state (as the Senate Chaplain periscope so well indicates), though never a Catholic one.

The heart of Pink's argument, moreover, echoes those of several Pontiffs who maintained that, in some decisive way, without "grace" and perhaps other supernatural help or ecclesiastical ministrations – or both – even the most reasonable human persons could not effectively promote the common good. Pink quotes Pope Pius IX, who warned in *Quanta Cura* that "where religion has been removed from civil society, and the doctrine and authority of divine revelation repudiated, the genuine notion itself of justice and human right is darkened and lost." He quotes Pope Leo XII to similar effect. He does not quote Pope Saint Pius X, who wrote in his condemnation of the French Silonists, "[T]here is no true civilization without its being moral civilization, and there is no true moral civilization without the true religion: this is a truth demonstrated; it is a fact of history."

That "[h]uman reason requires repair through grace" is the root claim in this part of the integralist case. The challenge to the integralists, though, is to show how that salve can be applied to the "state," save by and through the reasoning (influenced by grace) of the *persons* who exercise public authority. That they, along with all human persons, should come to Catholic faith, is an end devoutly to be prayed for. But this great good must be brought about *seriatim,* and by appeal to each one's freedom and intelligence. *That* is the legacy of Madison and the founding, of *DH*, and indeed of the Gospel. In other words, public servants (as all others) *need to be converted.* Again, it is not clear what exactly a Catholic "confession" by the "state" would add to what seems, on other solid grounds, to be already shown to be sound.

It might be supposed that this process could be jumpstarted, and the halcyon influence of the Church accelerated, by "establishing" Catholicism. It is impossible to say for sure. But it is certain that "grace" does not work automatically, as the depredations of so many officially Catholic kingdoms and states throughout history sadly make clear. It might instead be that at or just below the surface of the integralists' arguments is a deeply conservative social theory, one in which the doctrine of the Church, the supernatural incentives of the faith, and the cultural authority of the clergy, are all thought to be essential to adequate peace and order. This is not an altogether implausible claim. But it is not nearly obviously correct. The burden of showing that it is true rests upon those who assert that it is so. In the meantime, Catholics clerical and lay should bear perspicuous witness to the truth in season and out of season, and never lose their grip on all the truths which they hold.

Conclusion

Properly understood, the American constitutional tradition provides the foundations in moral and religious truth necessary to anchor the true common good of our political society. A Catholic "establishment" would not necessarily be unjust, so long as ample provision was made for the religious liberty of everyone, in accord with the grounds, scope, and limits articulated in *DH*.

The First Amendment as correctly understood, however, (and much more as it is interpreted today), blocks recognition of Catholicism as the true religion. To this important but limited extent, integralism is not a possibility in the United States, neither in the past nor in a hypothetical, optimistically projected, future. The difference between integralism (meaning a Catholic "confessional state") and the moral and religious truth which *is* to be recognized is not great, save for my perplexity, expressed earlier in this chapter, about the prospect of "grace" entering into the pursuit of the common good except by and through the choices and actions of persons who exercise public authority. At least this much is certain: Catholics and other Americans can do inestimable good for their society and its laws without taking on the burden of advocating for a Catholic establishment.

Chapter 4
When Do People Begin?

Abortion is the great civil rights issue of our time. One reason is that the lives of a million human persons are at stake. Per year. Think of it this way: if even only a tiny fraction – say one percent – of those persons killed in abortion annually was instead killed by the Border Patrol as they tried to illegally enter the country, or by municipal police officers in adversarial street encounters, the carnage would be front page news every day, all day. Any political aspirant who failed to pledge to *immediately* end the killing of that one percent – approximately ten thousand migrants or inner-city residents – would be a non-starter. Stopping the killing would surely be the nation's number one priority.

For a split-second someone might object to thinking of abortion this way. This objector might say that, of course, those examples are shocking. The public outcry would indeed be unquenchable. But the killers in those examples are *public* police officers, and the *state* most certainly must not do heinous things like that! It is different with abortion, this line of thought would continue, because with abortion it is a matter of ensuring women's privacy *from* an intrusive state. Besides, to prohibit wanton police killings is just to insist that the government treat all persons as equal bearers of a right to life. To prohibit abortion is, in effect, to foist on everyone a particular answer to the question: when do people begin? Our objector would then conclude that justice requires the state to permit each pregnant woman to decide that matter for herself.

Does it? To legally prohibit abortion does mean that lawmakers have taken a stand on when people begin (in the case of abortion, that people begin at fertilization). But that is true of *all* homicide laws. The spare language of a typical murder statute, for instance, is this: "It shall be murder if one person intentionally kills another person".[1] There never has been and never will be a homicide prosecution that does not take a stand on whether the victim was really a *person*, no matter how old (or young) or how debilitated (or well) that person was. Most pro-abortion people accept, moreover, that laws against killing newborns are a requirement of justice. Those laws surly involve taking a stand about when people begin – no later than birth – and "imposing" it on everybody, whether they like it or not.

Is there really *any* morally significant difference between the police killings and abortion? Let's say that instead of the Border Patrol or municipal police, a group of irate misguided ranchers (at the border) and a citizens' neighborhood security patrol (in the city) did the killing, while the government stood idly by, except to block by force anyone who tried to step in and stop the ranchers and vigilantes. Would the public demands for an immediate end to the killing be any less fervent?

I doubt it.

The truth is that "respect life from the moment of conception" is not advice only for private persons or solely for the government. It is a requirement of justice binding on both! Pope John II wrote, "[t]he negative precepts of the natural moral law are universally valid. They oblige each and every individual, always and in every circumstance ... It is prohibited – to everyone and in every case – to violate these precepts. They oblige everyone, regardless of the cost" (*Veritatis splendor* 52).

The epochal injustice of abortion, then, does not depend on anything controversial about the ethics of killing. It depends entirely on whether the unborn *count* as persons.

I

Abortion is the great civil rights issue of our time for another reason. It raises – uniquely and compellingly – the foundational question about law

---

1   Either in a murder statute itself or somewhere nearby there will be an exception to the basic prohibition for "justified" use of lethal force, where one person reasonably apprehends that another person is, in plain terms, trying to kill them and uses deadly force to defend himself or herself. This exception is just. It would pertain to abortions procured to save a mother's life. It does not pertain to and would not "justify" all but a tiny number of abortions performed annually in America.

and justice that every society must face. "When do people begin?" is the same question as: *Who* is the law for? For *whose* benefit do we plan and build and apply this vast apparatus we call the "the law"? The question is foundational because it is prior, in status and importance, to the question: what shall the law be? It is foundational also because answering it right is essential to justice. Anyone can see that even an exquisitely balanced scaffolding of legal rights and duties counts for naught, if the strong can with impunity manipulate the question, and use the law to subjugate those whom they wish to exploit. It is hardly justice if the aristocrats treat each other with exquisite courtesy and respect, while they all grind the serfs into dust.

Jurists as far back as Justinian in the sixth century correctly saw that law is for *persons,* not the other way around. Persons are the point of law. Law is their servant. Persons are not for the state, or for the fatherland, or for the glory of the common law. These personal beneficiaries are not to be identified through policy analysis. They are not the sums of interests balanced or of the foreseeable effects of choosing to recognize some class of human beings as persons, or not. The older jurists saw, too, that the question of "personhood" could not be an intra-systemic riddle, solved by a feat of technical legal reasoning, and answered with a legal fiction, or term of art – as if the law could be as impervious to the reality of persons as Chancery was to justice in Dickens' fabled case of *Jaundice v. Jaundice.* In *Bleak House,* as well as in *Roe v. Wade,* such legal churning amounts to pettifoggery.

Being prior to law and indispensable to justice, the foundational question of when people begin must be answered according to the truth of matter: everyone who really is a person counts in law as one. The law is for everyone who is a person, and that is it. "When do people begin?" is therefore inescapably a question most unforgiving of wrong answers.

The most important provision in our fundamental law – the Constitution – is its guarantee to all "persons" of the "equal protection of the laws." All our legal rights and privileges depend on it. None of our rights and privileges would be secure if some people – those with the most money or power or those who complain the loudest – could arrange for other people not to count in law *as* "persons." Slavery was one such arrangement. Slaveholders did not altogether deny that slaves were human persons. Slaveholders could see that slaves were reasoning beings, possessed of volition. Many slaveholders recognized slaves' humanity by according them religious instruction and respecting their family affairs. (Many did not.) All slaveholders denied, though, that slaves enjoyed legal rights. A slave could never demand in court legal equality with his or her master. Slaves were persons whom the law treated for the sake of their masters. Slaves were their owners' *property*.

Most people need little help from the law to value their own sakes over the fortunes of others, especially those not bound to them by blood or affinity. The allure of manipulating others is eminently understandable. One's life goes easier when one can instrumentalize other persons to one's own projects, ends, goals, needs. Where the law fails to restrain such manipulation, where it sanctions subordination of some for the sake of others, great injustice results. In the wake of injustice comes rationalizations, then later an ideology of inequality. Before long a whole culture of subordination grows up, as feminists and pro-lifers and those who speak for African-Americans have been right to remind us.

II

Now, to ask the right question is not straightaway to get the right answer. Serious and good people have sometimes been wrong about when persons begin, due (for example) to their misunderstanding of human reproduction. Knowing nothing of egg and sperm, Thomas Aquinas famously thought that people began about forty days into a pregnancy when movement within the womb is first detected. Thomas's society sanctioned injustices, for which these misguided people bore no subjective guilt and, crucially, which their openness to the truth about people and their commitment to doing justice to everyone, permitted them to eventually get right. It is entirely another matter to say that the law is opaque to, and even uninterested in, the truth about when persons begin.

Put differently: it is gravely unjust to expose a class of (real) persons to the wanton violence of other people. It is wrong to get the answer to the foundational question wrong, even if (as with Thomas) there is an exculpatory explanation for doing so. But it is an epic injustice and grossly culpable to suppress the question about when people begin altogether, so that the stronger can exploit the defenseless without obstruction by the truth.

Clear-headed jurists through the centuries would therefore have shuddered at the legal philosopher Ronald Dworkin's argument that the question about "persons" is like a membership application to the Rotary Club: do those who already count want to open up the rolls? They would have been staggered by John Rawls' argument that the "just" abortion policy for America is that which respects the right of everyone in the argument to be heard respectfully. They would naturally have rejected President Obama's message on the 2012 anniversary of *Roe,* when he said: "[W]e must ...continue our efforts to ensure that our daughters have the same rights, freedoms, and opportunities as our sons to fulfill their dreams." The President was speaking, utterly without irony, only of those sons and daughters who survived the womb. Besides, no one's son has anything like the "rights, freedom, and opportunities" of everyone's daughters, when it come to the life or death of *their* child. Justinian and his successors would have been horrified by the pettifoggery of the *Roe* Court, which set upon the foundational question of when people begin with the zeal of a clerk, and with the charity of a pirate.

III

In *Roe v. Wade* the Supreme Court expressly, and repeatedly, declined to "resolve the difficult question of when life begins." That case was decided upon the curious basis that states could not deny a pregnant woman choice about abortion by imposing what the Court called "one theory of life" upon her – without first (or at any point) taking up the burden of ascertaining whether that choice would be homicidal. The Court blithely catalogued seven "detriments" (the Court's word) of denying pregnant women that choice. Tellingly, only one of the seven had to do with carrying a child in the womb: "medically diagnosable harm" during pregnancy. The other "detriments" had to do with anticipated burdens of raising a child. These challenges of child-rearing included (in *Roe's* words) the prospect that "[m]aternity, or additional offspring, may force upon the woman a distressful life and future." In addition, "[p]sychological harm may be imminent. Mental and physical health may be taxed by child care. There is also the distress, for all concerned, associated with the unwanted child, and there is the problem of bringing a child into a family already unable, psychologically and otherwise, to care for it." Only one of these post-natal "detriments" is distinctive to women.

The reasoning of *Roe* would lead without further ado to a right to commit infanticide, were the reasons for abortion (the seven "detriments") not stopped cold by "a theory of life," one which holds that people begin *at least no later than at birth.* Make no mistake about it, too: *nowhere* does the United States Constitution say or imply that persons begin at birth. That conviction has to be imported into constitutional law, carried there by reflections upon scientific and biological facts, analyzed and weighed in light of reason and logic. Were such a "theory of life" not supplied to our law by truth-seeking and justice-loving people, it would be advisable for us all to make sure that our doors are locked and the alarms set every night.

The Justices were allergic to the pivotal question of when people really begin. During *Roe's* pendency Justice William Brennan wrote in a memorandum to Justice Douglas that "moral predilections must not be allowed to influence our minds in setting legal distinctions," here quoting Tom Clark who quoted Oliver Wendell Homes. "The law deals in reality not obscurity – the known rather than the unknown. The law does not deal in speculation." Clark opined that because the fetus "cannot interact with other human beings . . . there is no proof of life in the sense that the law contemplates proof of fact." *Roe* concluded that the state may not "by adopting one theory of life override the rights of the pregnant women that are at stake."

The Catholic Church and its moral opposition to abortion unwittingly helped the *Roe* majority chart its path. University of Virginia law professor John Jeffries, one of Justice Lewis Powell's former clerks, explained that "the idea that a fertilized embryo was a fully recognized life would always seem to him unacceptably remote from ordinary experience. That this belief was closely associated with the Catholic Church only made it easier for him to dismiss. No argument would have persuaded Powell that the disturbing realities of unwanted pregnancy and back-alley abortion should be subordinated to religious dogma."

I do not know who else on the *Roe* Court shared Powell's identification of anti-abortion sentiment with the Church's "dogma." Justice William Douglas likely did, and others might have. The important point is that the

Court bought into – really, created for the occasion – an ersatz epistemological framework, which pitted the hard "reality" of unwanted parenting against a speculative idea or theory or doctrine or "dogma" – all matters of unverifiable opinion – about when people begin.

IV

On this point there was no disagreement on the *Roe* Court, notwithstanding that Justices Rehnquist and White dissented from the Court's striking holding in favor of abortion. Nor has there been any disagreement on the Court since. No one who has served on the Court since 1973 – including Justices who surely are convinced that people really begin at fertilization – has *ever* stated in an opinion that the *Roe* Court erred by failing to declare that the truth about persons is the key to applying the Constitution's guarantee of equal protection to "all *persons*."

It is here worth pausing over this characteristic limitation of the standing alternative to "identity" jurisprudence. Although "conservative" civil liberties thinking is vastly preferable to the derailment initiated by the Mystery Passage, it is still a flawed methodology. "Conservative" jurisprudence is properly guided by strategic recourse to historical sources such as the "original" public understanding of the Constitution. But it is too skeptical of moral reasoning in law to get the job at hand done right each time. Again, "conservative" constitutionalism in particular very often produces the correct result in cases. But its foundations are insufficiently moral. Its roots are *too* historical, *too* conventional, *too* restricted, and *too* averse to unrestricted moral (and metaphysical) reasoning to handle the challenge of contemporary Mystery-Passage civil liberties.

The saddest example of this deficiency is abortion. The nearly universal "conservative" answer to the question posed in *Roe v Wade* is that the Constitution is agnostic about abortion *and about fetal rights*. Justices whom we have every reason to believe are as pro-life as could be nonetheless hold that the Constitution reserves the whole question to the fifty states: if California wants to have abortion-on-demand, this answer explains, Californians are at liberty to have it. These jurists ignore the obvious challenge – in fact, their duty – to supply some meaning to the constitutional subjects of "equal protection of the laws" against homicide – "persons"!

V

Perhaps one could partially defend the reasoning of *Roe* and the reticence of conservatives along lines indicated by the Justices then and since: the Court in *Roe* tried, honestly it might be alleged, to do the right *legal* thing. For that reason they hewed closely to the facts of maternal distress and treated the "persons" to whom the Constitution guaranteed "equal protection of the laws" as a technical legal term, whose meaning was to be mined from within the four corners of the Constitution.

This is exactly the *opposite* of what the Constitution itself plainly requires. To what I have already said in this chapter, I would add that when the Fourteenth Amendment refers to "persons," it points to and incorporates a moral reality. That is the most natural reading of the term "any person." That is what the strictly legal materials direct the judicial interpreter to do! The only way to make sense of the amendment is to understand "person" as an exhaustive reference to a natural kind. Anyone can see that the aspiration to equality could be nullified, if public authority could "define" some human individuals as non-persons.

The historical record confirms these general considerations. Ohio Representative John Bingham sponsored the Fourteenth Amendment in the House of Representatives. During debate over what is now Section 1, he said that its coverage was "universal." It applied, Bingham declared, to "any human being." Congressman Bingham's counterpart in the Senate, Senator Jacob Howard, emphasized that the amendment applied to every member of the human family.

Newspaper coverage of the debate included references like "all men," "all persons," and "all men as equals before the law of God and man." Addressing a large crowd on July 18, 1866, Indiana Governor Oliver Morton declared that Section 1 "intended to throw the equal personal and proprietary protection of the law around every person who may be within the jurisdiction of the state." Two weeks later the *New York Times* said, "The equal protection of the laws is guaranteed to all, without any exception."

The prevailing spirit is captured in the opinion of an Iowa court, handed down in 1868, the year of the Fourteenth Amendment's ratification: The common law is "to be commended for its all-embracing and salutary solicitude for the sacredness of human life and the personal safety of every human being." The court wrote that this "protecting, paternal care envelop[s] every individual like the air he breathes," and it "not only extends to persons actually born, but for some purposes to infants *in ventre sa mere.*"

VI

Hard cold scientific facts which have been confirmed or in some instances uncovered since 1973 make *Roe's* aversion to speculating about when people begin untenable. That abortion kills a person with a right to life has become easier to see since *Roe v. Wade.* Progress in scientific research and medical practice has made both birth and "viability" nearly unbelievable grounds for demarcating between "human life" demanding moral respect, and mere "potential life" which has no traction in justice against a mother's desires. The near-ubiquity of sonograms has probably done more to convince the popular mind that a real baby comes to be by ten weeks into pregnancy than intellectual arguments for fetal personhood have. Earlier and earlier pre-natal medical interventions for the sake of the unborn patient confirm this impression. DNA indubitably confirms the substantial biological iden-tity of the embryo with the human being whose features anyone can detect as early as at ten weeks. Cogent philosophical argument confirms what com-mon sense operating on all this (and other) data so strongly suggests: not only that a distinct human individual comes to be at fertilization, but that this individual is substantially the same as the individual (with an as-yet undoubted right-not-to-be-killed) who is born nine months later, is brought home from the hospital days after that, and so on throughout that person's earthly life.

To the objection by some and the worry by others that these restrictions represent a "bridge to far" – that neither the law nor the American people are ready to recognize the unborn as "persons" with the same right not-to-be-killed that other people have – the answer is simple: it has *already* hap-pened. Thirty-eight states and the federal government have enacted what are commonly called "feticide" laws. These homicide statutes protect the child *in utero* from being killed and punish those who violate them in the same way that the law punishes the killing of anybody else. (Scott Peterson, now imprisoned in San Quentin for killing his wife Lacy and unborn son Connor, is just one of many people, almost all of them men, who are serving time for feticide.) These laws all include an exception for lawful abortions, as *Roe* dictates. Otherwise they recognize the truth about when people begin. They commit the law to the full protection of persons at their beginning which justice requires.

VII

The future of the American anti-abortion movement lies in restrictions founded upon the unborn person's right to life. This is not to say that activists need to have *something* to do and that other avenues are blocked. Fetal right-to-life *should* be anti-abortionists' focus, because the fundamental and unvarying wrong in abortion is not slipshod medical practice or unintelligent assent – troubling as those contingent and common evils are – but *killing*. Other bases for abortion restrictions are honorable and sound. In my judgment, however, restrictions upon abortion strictly as a medical procedure, and others rooted in the need to be sure that there is "informed consent" by the pregnant woman, have just about run their course. The way forward now is to emphasize the unborn victims of abortion.

Conscientious legislators and citizens should continue to enact abortion restrictions premised upon the personhood of the unborn. As a matter of fact, they have recently enacted in many American states two types of abortion restrictions for the sake of the unborn as rights-bearing persons. One type involves prohibitions which recognize that the fetus is a person "well before birth," and even before "viability." Examples include bans after the point of "fetal pain" (at about twenty weeks), and "fetal heartbeat" prohibitions after about eight weeks. Both these sets of laws include exceptions for abortions necessary to preserve the life of the mother or her physical health against severe injury. They all represent attempts to more or less align abortion regulation with the scope of morally justified killing of one person by another.

Conclusion

Most living Americans cannot personally recall the world before January 22, 1973, when the Supreme Court in *Roe v. Wade* forced abortion-on-demand upon every state in the country. Many Americans old enough to remember that day welcomed the decision. Today one of the two major political parties – the one which historically has been the home of America's Catholics – makes full-throated support for *Roe* a non-negotiable requirement for any national candidate. These Americans think easy access to abortion, government subsidized if necessary, should be part of this nation's civic fabric.

To its great credit, the pro-life movement has persisted since 1973 in preserving the spirit of justice for everyone, and in promoting a willingness to face the demands of the truth unafraid. The fruits of this effort, along with the revelations of neonatal and genetic science and some signal legal successes, provide reason to hope that by courageously pressing the truth home to Americans' consciences in season and out of season, many, many lives will be saved.

Abortion is not only the great civil rights issue of our time. It is the greatest human rights tragedy in America's history. Sixty million people have been killed in lawful abortions since *Roe*. That is a hundred times the number of Americans killed in combat during World War II. That is many millions more than all the persons enslaved in the course of American history. For the entire year of 2018 Americans killed twenty-five people via capital punishment. Every fifteen minutes that year Americans killed that many people by abortion.

Roe seems to many people now to be an experiment too big – too ingrained, too institutionalized—to fail. In truth, the question of when people begin is too important to get wrong.

Chapter 5
The Truth about the Family

"Many who deem same-sex marriage to be wrong reach that conclusion based on decent and honorable religious or philosophical premises, and neither they nor their beliefs are disparaged here." So said the Supreme Court, speaking through Justice Anthony Kennedy, on June, 26, 2015. In the case of *Obergefell v Hodges,* a bare five-member majority mandated that day that civil marriage be made available to same-sex couples "on the same terms and conditions as opposite-sex couples."

Anthony Kennedy has since retired from the Court, replaced by one of his own former law clerks in 2018. Brett Kavanaugh's Senate confirmation hearing was a brutal exercise in sexual politics. Almost any American reader (and quite a few others) will easily recall the turmoil about Christine Blasey Ford's allegation that, decades earlier, Kavanaugh sexually assaulted her at a high-school party. Neil Gorsuch (who also happened to clerk for Anthony Kennedy) has ascended to the Supreme Court since *Obergefell,* too. He replaced one of the four *Obergefell* dissenting Justices, the deceased Antonin Scalia.

Since 2015 the Court has decided just one case – *Pavan v. Smith,* in 2017 – where the decision necessarily affirmed the *Obergefell* ruling. In *Pavan* the Court invalidated an Arkansas law which said that, when a married woman gives birth, the name of the woman's husband is entered on the child's birth certificate because he is legally presumed to be the father. For obvious biological reasons, Arkansas did not accord the same presumption of "paternity" to a lesbian birth mother's female spouse. The Court, over the strong objections of Justices Thomas, Alito, and Gorsuch, held that Arkansas acted in violation of *Obergefell.* The state would have to find a way to treat male and female spouses exactly the same way, even when it comes to "paternity."

The Supreme Court's doctrines about what the lawyers call *stare decisis*, or the practice of following rules established in previous cases, are unsettled and contentious and closely watched from outside the Court. The reason why even average citizens care about *stare decisis* has nothing to do with the matter's intrinsic interest, though. It is because any high court discussion of how to honor precedent could signal the fate of *Roe v Wade*. Many millions of Americans care greatly about that!

As a general matter and apart from abortion, a Supreme Court precedent just a few years old, decided by a 5-4 vote, bitterly resented by four Justices when it was decided, and affirmed just once since, would be a ripe candidate for reconsideration at an early opportunity. Add in the personnel changes to the Court since 2015, and one might well expect that *Obergefell* is up for grabs. One could tally up all the indicators: three *Obergefell* dissenters remain on the Court – Justices Samuel Alito, Clarence Thomas, and Chief Justice John Roberts. Their dissenting opinions were as caustic as any in recent memory. (Equally so was the late Scalia's opinion). It is impossible to say for sure. But it is very probable that there is now a majority on the Court which would *not* have decided *Obergefell* as the Court did.

Legalized same-sex "marriage" is nonetheless here to stay. Even assuming that a majority of the present Court believe that *Obergefell* was wrongly decided, the Court is not going to reverse that case. I leave aside the reasons why that is so, in order to ask the crucially important question: what should those who hold the "decent and honorable" conviction that marriage between two men or between two women is simply impossible do now?

It is tempting for those who resisted same-sex civil "marriage" to conclude that it is time to move on. It is also understandable, especially since it is here to stay. These good but discouraged people would say that it is time to circle the cultural wagons, seek sufficient legal space to carry on for themselves the sacred tradition about marriage, do what they can to pass it along to their children, and hopefully be able to do these things without having to retreat behind the figurative walls of the monastery or into a new Catholic ghetto.

I think that, for *all these reasons*, it is instead time to double-down on the truth about marriage and the family built upon it. It is time to promote it aggressively in the public square, not in a defensive posture seeking to be left alone, but precisely *as* the truth for everyone. Defending publicly and robustly the truth about marriage and family is essential to keeping it alive in our minds as something worth choosing, to giving those who choose real marriage a fair chance at succeeding in it, to transmitting it to the next generation, to clearing space enough to live peaceably within its light, to preserving religious liberty for wedding vendors as well as for religious institutions, and to preserving the civil liberty that marriage and the family inescapably require in our society.

In other words, the way forward is to *sustain* those "decent and honorable premises" as decent and honorable, especially as *philosophical* truths. We have already seen in this book how fragile "religious" premises are. We saw especially in the first two chapters how they are practically synonymous with "irrational" and "subjective. Down that path is utter marginalization. Therein lies the trap set for the truth by enthusiasts for the new liberationist order: opposition to same-sex marriage is owed no more respect, and deserves no more quarter, than does opposition to interracial marriage.

I

Justice Alito's brilliant dissenting opinion in *Obergefell* provides the map. He saw clearly that behind the brute force of the majority opinion was the five Justices' adherence to a strictly companionate view of marriage: "Although the Court expresses the point in loftier terms, its argument is that the fundamental purpose of marriage is to promote the well-being of those who choose to marry. . . . This understanding of marriage, which focuses almost entirely on the happiness of persons who choose to marry, is shared by many people today." Alito recognized that this view is "not the traditional one. For millennia, marriage was inextricably linked to the one thing that only an opposite-sex couple can do: procreate." Those states which limit legal marriage to opposite-sex couples do so, Alito said, because marriage, unlike other fulfilling human relationships, "encourage[s] potentially procreative conduct to take place within a lasting unit that has long been thought to provide the best atmosphere for raising children."

Yes, the fundamental distinguishing feature of true marriage is its *essential* – defining, necessary – orientation to procreation. If that is not true, then opposition to same-sex "marriage" really is arbitrary, as Alito implied. Defending the truth about marriage is largely a matter of defending its essential connection to procreation.

How is that possible? Many people objected to the procreative-meaning argument during the fight over same-sex "marriage." They asked: how could laws limiting marriage to the male-female couple be justified by an asserted link between marriage and procreation, if some opposite-sex couples who are unable or unwilling to have children are nonetheless free to enter state-recognized marriages? After all, as many judges observed, the elderly and the sterile are legally permitted to marry. They concluded – fallaciously – that procreation could not possibly be the point of marriage. They concluded, in other words, that because some sterile couples may legally marry, marriage itself is sterile.

One state judge wrote shortly before *Obergefell* that "many heterosexual couples" are allowed to marry even though they do not have "the intent or ability to naturally procreate children." One federal circuit court wrote: "The elderly, those medically unable to conceive, and those who exercise their fundamental right not to have biological children are free to marry … apparently without breaking the 'conceptual link' [identified by the state] between marriage and procreation."

Let's call this "the infertility objection" to traditional marriage law's dependence upon an essential orientation to procreation.

There was nothing new about it in the run-up to *Obergefell*. In 1971 in a case called *Baker v. Nelson*, homosexual plaintiffs argued "that the state does not impose upon heterosexual married couples a condition that they have a proved capacity or declared willingness to procreate." The Minnesota Supreme Court rejected the "infertility" argument in *Baker*. The United States Supreme Court summarily affirmed that decision a year later, stating that the case did not even present a substantial federal question.

What's new about the infertility objection is that courts became so beguiled by it. I say "beguiled" here advisedly, because these courts typically stopped thinking once the infertility objection was made. They chanted their confident agreement with the slogan – "It cannot be procreation because elderly people are permitted to marry!" – and proceeded with haste to invalidate marriage laws which dated from time out-of-mind, which had been sanctioned by all the world religions, and which until the day before yesterday were unquestioned within American society and law.

Here are some examples of this judicial mindlessness. Courts sometimes said that the asserted link between procreation and marriage is "definitional," and thus (they further said) "circular." It is hard to make sense of this criticism. Definitions are not "circular" or "linear" or anything directional or graphical, save in the limited sense that one must first have some idea of what one is trying to define, before one tries to define it. This is true of *all* definitions, including those of natural entities (lemons and llamas) as well as existential/moral entities (families and football teams). These courts might really have been trying to say that the states' lawyers begged the question by relying upon an *undefended* definition of marriage. But the states in these cases *did* defend their understanding of marriage, albeit not convincingly to these ideologically intoxicated judges.

These courts might instead have meant that "definitions" of marriage are misplaced in lawsuits, because all such accounts are fantastical or strictly theological or somehow for each couple to settle for their own relationships. In other words, courts might have been trying to say that defining marriage as a male-female union is basically *arbitrary*. But these same courts then – often in the exact same paragraph – *defined* marriage as the "mutual," "lasting," "intimate" "commitment" of the "two" spouses. These courts effectively took over the state's definition of marriage, save for its essential link to procreation. Who is being "arbitrary" now?

Some judges and Justices took over the *Baker* plaintiffs' position. These jurists maintained that linking marriage to procreation implies or entails that – somehow – infertile opposite-sex couples must be identified and barred from legal marriage, on pain of fatal contradiction. This thought seems to be that minimally honorable legislators would not, or at least should not be permitted by judges to, stipulate a definition of marriage unless they see to a perfect fit between the defining characteristic – a "procreative" union of male and female – and the roster of married couples in that state. But this type of extraordinary fit between legislative purpose and the operational reach of a law is *not* required in *any* area of our constitutional law.

Most tellingly, courts which defined marriage as the "lasting" "intimate" "loving" "mutual commitment" of any two partners never suggested that the relevant public authority must inquire, interrogate, or otherwise vet the two persons to whom a marriage license issues, to be certain that they *really* love each other, *truly* provide mutual support, *genuinely* intend to stay together permanently, or *ever* intend to have sex with each other. These courts' argument is radically defective: if it were sound it would either exclude their own idea of what marriage is, or it would imply that no marriage laws could pass constitutional muster.

In any event, how would the state vet couples for fertility? Should engaged men and women have to submit to the medical tests necessary to ascertain, to a reasonable degree of scientific certainty, that each is in good working order? Should couples be required to swear (affirm under penalty of perjury) that they intend to procreate? If so, is there to be a date certain for the happy event, after which their marriage license is revoked? Revocation, too, for married couples who try to have kids, but cannot do so because of infertility arising *after* their wedding? What about an engaged couple who say that they are uncertain about kids? Or that they are "open" to the prospect? May they marry, or not? As the Minnesota court in *Baker* rightly suggested, *any* such regimen is bound to be both "unrealistic" and "offensive," and would likely invade couples' constitutionally protected privacy.

Consider now the law pertaining to another basic requirement of marriage. Entering into marriage obviously requires a certain level of maturity, along with a robust willingness to settle the future course of one's life. Otherwise, the legal requirement that anyone marrying do so with knowing and free consent would be a joke. Even so, the law does not run a battery of tests to ascertain any aspiring couples' reflectiveness, or immaturity. Getting a marriage license is no more complicated than registering a car. In each case you just need to be eighteen, and willing.

One could well say about the age and gender pre-requisites that the state *presumes* maturity and fertility of men and women over eighteen. One could say of each prerequisite that the law relies upon it as a more or less adequate *proxy* for the more precise relevant quality (of responsibility and fertility). One could say that these proxies satisfy the state's educative obligations towards marriage, by signaling in *general terms* what marriage is really about. One could say that the law *goes as far as it reasonably can* in limiting marriage to those who are mature and interested in having kids. Once could say that, were the state to attempt more rigor, it would *violate* the couples' legal rights and legitimate privacy expectations.

One could – and should – say *all* these things. For all these reasons, the *Baker* court rightly said that "the classification is no more than theoretically imperfect." Abstract symmetry is not demanded by the Constitution. Or by common sense and justice.

As a matter of fact, because men can father children well into old age, the only imaginable categorical exception to traditional marriage laws would be marriages to which a surely post-menopausal woman – say, aged fifty-five or over – is a party. But that would not be a rational exception to make. For some of these women will be widows with young children, perhaps born to them between the ages of forty to forty-five. These women might well be marrying to give their children the nearest approximation available to the maternal/paternal family upbringing which the state's laws do what they can to bring into being for all children. This could be true of widows with children up to age eighteen, so that the state would have no reason to prohibit, and ample reason to promote, at least some marriages of women up to around age sixty.

Conversely, some women beyond the age of fertility will be marrying aged widowers with young or not-so-young children. These men might marry older women for the same reason that older widows might marry them: to give children still in the home a close approximation of family life. Besides, some older infertile couples marry with a view to adopting and bringing up, or simply of fostering, children, perhaps the grandchildren or other relatives of one or both of them.

That leaves only unions involving elderly women who marry for the first time, where the couple have no existing children and do not intend to adopt or foster any, as a candidate "class" for exclusion from state-recognized marriage. Let's call these couples "free riders." But any of these couples could subsequently decide to adopt or foster. For that reason alone the state possesses a reason to sanction their unions. Most elderly couples are "childless" anyway, in that they are empty-nesters. Some others married young but were never blessed with the children they desired to have.

That a few of all the "childless" elderly couples around town are actually "free riders" would be, perhaps, generally assumed. But few people would know *which* couples. And their presence among a much larger population of married opposite-sex couples would be no scandal. It would call for no re-definition of what legal marriage is about, as legal recognition of same-sex relationships as marriages surely would. The state has no interest in amending its legal prerequisites for marriage in an effort to disqualify this residual and undetectable class of "free riders."

When all is said and done, it is plainly the case that conscientious legislators who believe that marriage is essentially oriented to procreation would do *exactly* what our laws have always done, namely, limit it to consenting men and women. Our country's laws as they were and still as they should be, *presumed* that opposite-sex couples who wish to marry are fertile, in roughly the way that the law presumes maturity and capacity to consent of anyone who is eighteen or older.

The civil law of marriage is not any time soon going to return to its pre-*Obergefell* soundness. But refuting the infertility fallacy is nonetheless crucial to properly educating young people (especially) about the meaning of marriage, to keeping the truth about marriage alive, and to passing it on in deed and word, is a serious moral obligation. Maintaining clarity about the truth that marriage is essentially procreative is essential to retaining respect for it as a "decent and honorable religious and philosophical" position, lest those who hold and act on it be further relegated to the pariah status of unthinking bigots. Refuting this specious objection is, in other words, necessary to keeping up the "decent and honorable" philosophical belief that marriage is reserved to the union of one man and one woman.

II

Recall that Justice Alito wrote in his *Obergefell* dissent that "marriage, unlike other fulfilling human relationships ... encourage[s] potentially procreative conduct to take place within a lasting unit that has long been thought to provide *the best atmosphere for raising children*" (emphasis added).

There are two very different senses to "best atmosphere" in the context of Alito's remark. One of them (which I believe Alito had specifically in mind) was the central argument made by friends of marriage in the battle against the same-sex counterfeit of it. Much of the argument made by both sides of the debate in legislatures, in courts, and in the marketplace of ideas about legal recognition of same-sex "marriages" was about how well children do in various sorts of households. The arguments centered on social scientific comparisons of homes headed by same-sex couples compared to mother-and-father homes. These studies identified sundry indicia of well-being, such as academic achievement, truancy rates, reported self-esteem, and ability to make friends. These are good things. But they are not measures of human flourishing in any morally significant sense. The class valedictorian could be a rotten kid. Troubled students are often very good people. The most popular girl in the high school can be the worst brat – and so on.

Friends of marriage promoted studies which tended to show that there *was* a difference, one in favor of opposite-sex households. They argued (correctly) that the "no-difference" or "just-as-good" studies of same-sex households up to *Obergefell* were so limited in their sample size, or so flawed in other ways, that they were seriously defective. Some were actually worthless pieces of advocacy junk science. The number of reliable studies establishing a statistically significant deficit of child well-being in same-sex households is smaller. But some of these – most notably one by University of Texas scholar Mark Regnerus – were quite probative as social science. It was highly suggestive of what thorough and unbiased work of this sort would show.

This strategic choice by friends of marriage was nonetheless an unfortunate one. One problem was that the good social science could not deliver anything like the pay-off that defenders of true marriage wanted. Nothing like a *conclusive* social science case against same-sex "marriage" parenting was ever in the offing. The studies tended to show a statistically significant benefit to being in an opposite-sex household. But the differences were not great. Obviously, many children who are in same-sex homes do better than many children who are not. What friends of marriage usually called "optimal setting" (Alito's "best atmosphere") was a gross measure which did not purport to identify what is best for *this* child or whether *those* prospective parents would be successful, so measured.

Besides, if two men could in truth marry, then the state should not prohibit them from doing so, even if some cohort of which they are members bears a slight statistical deficit according to some important aspects of psychological or emotional well-being for potential children. On the other hand, if two men cannot really marry, then for that reason the law should not permit them to do so. Either way the prospects for children play no role in a sound approach to how the state should approach and regulate marriage. Indeed, no one suggests – well, one hopes that no one suggests – that certain opposite-sex cohorts, say, couples without any college attendance or where one has a criminal conviction or where each is a child of divorced or alcoholic parents or where one or both was raised in trailer park, not be permitted to marry because *statistically* such couples turn out more maladjusted kids than, for example, an educated same-sex couple.

In addition: the whole "optimal setting" argument is not an argument against same-sex marriage at all. All that it tends to show – and that, crudely – is that same-sex couples should not be raising children. That is obviously a question distinct from whether they should be permitted to marry, for no such couple can bring children into the world by dint of being married; that is, by their "marital" sexual acts. Many same-sex couples "have" children. But they can only do so by adoption, fostering, surrogacy, and other third-party arrangements. *These* and not any question about marrying, *should be the focal point of government regulation if, or to the extent that, these coupes are not suitable parents.* Some of these ways of acquiring children (adoption, for example) are *already* so couple-specific that statistical analyses of a cohort are irrelevant. And the other methods (such as surrogacy) could, if there was the political will to do so, be regulated on a couple-by-couple basis as well.

Because no two men or two women produce issue, recognizing them as married would not commit the law to placing children in their care. Unlike the situation with opposite-sex couples, in which legal recognition of them as married implies (or licenses, if you will) their having and raising children, laws recognizing same-sex couples as married would not by themselves mean children. The law would have to take an additional, specifically child-focused, step before any children were placed in the care of a same-sex couples through agencies of foster care or adoption, or by a legally valid custody arrangement where one or both partners come to the marriage with children of his or her own by a previous relationship. Nothing in "optimal setting" thinking would prevent such placements.

In sum, the "optimal setting" studies do not work against same-sex "marriage" and they are irrelevant to the matter of same-sex couples' rearing of children.

III

Friends of marriage unfortunately took their adversaries' bait. Skittish about making frankly moral arguments and stuck in what seemed to many of them to be a stalemate about the basic meaning of marriage ("companionate" versus "procreative"), they naturally sought what they hoped was a "neutral" work-around in social science. Rather than work forward from a defensible philosophical "premise" about what marriage is, they tried working backwards from a contingent matter of fact about what everyone could agree was a matter of great importance: the best-interests of the children. That this move by friends of marriage did not succeed does not establish that it was a mistaken strategy. But it *did* fail. It was also a radically unsound argument, with awful implications for how our polity should work with the truth about marriage and about legal regulation of who may marry. It is time now to rely upon the truth about marriage and the family founded upon it.

Here is a go at expressing that truth.

When the spouses' marital acts bear the fruit of children, these children are perceptively called *in the law* "issue of the marriage." To be sure, that is *not* what the overjoyed mom and dad tweet to their loved ones from the delivery room. She does not write: "Dearest friends, great news! Hubby and I just had an issue!" But "issue" has long been a term of art in legal accounts of the family, especially when it concerns inheritances and wills.

Leave that odd-sounding word aside if you like, and just consider the idea of children as simply *of* the marriage. This phrase alone signals the truth that children embody or actualize their parents' marriage. Just as the married couple is two-in-one-flesh, so too each child is the two-of-them-in-the one-flesh. The child comes to be *as* their marriage. He or she *is* their union. Each and every one of their offspring *is* the marriage of its mother and father – extended into time and space, and thus into human history and into the whole human community.

The truth is that children conceived in marital intercourse participate in the good of their parents' marriage and are themselves non-instrumental aspects of its perfection. They come to be as gifts that supervene upon the spouses' marital act. Thus, children are "of" the marriage, but they do not belong to the parents. They are not called forth "intentionally" to satisfy the parents' desires, objectives, or needs; much less are they manufactured as products, as they are in various sorts of assisted reproduction (IVF< or artificial insemination). When the spouses come together in the marital act, they give and receive themselves, a mutual exchange which may be blessed by a child's coming to be.

That child (and here I borrow language from a paper submitted by the Catholic Bishops of England some years ago to a Government Committee of Inquiry into in vitro fertilization), "although weak and dependent, enters the community of the family not as an object of production" or even as the satisfaction of parental intentions or objectives, "but as a kind of partner in the familial enterprise." The child comes to be on terms of "fundamental *parity* or *equality with* the parents."

Children come to be not only on terms of equal dignity with their parents. They come to be on similar terms with *each other* as well. Because all the married couple's children come to be in and through the *same* act – the marital act – separated only by time, all the children are equally and wholly the image (the embodiment, the expression) of their parents' unique union. The siblings' family identity is just that: a matter of *identity.* All the children are equally and wholly the offspring of the same parents; mother and father are equally and wholly parents of each child, in whom they see (literally) so many unique, yet related and, in a sense, identical expressions of their own union. For each child is their flesh, their marriage.

This web of familial equality, mutuality, and common identity is the wellspring of the love, duty, and loyalty that we see, and that we expect to find, among siblings. It is vital to emphasize here the complex matrix of connectedness, where biological unity yields a metaphysical oneness for the parents, whose two-in-one-flesh communion opens up to the gift of children, whose identities and status cement the sublime unity of that family. This unity includes the various moral duties that each family member owes to the others. But it also includes something else that even shirkers can never escape, namely, their *identity* as son or daughter of this mother and this father, and as sister or brother to these siblings with whom one shares not only relatives and memories. My brothers and sisters are *like me* in a way in which no other human person could be like me. My siblings are more than close friends with many shared experiences. They are part of me. We are each one of us imprints (actualizations) of the same unique marriage.

The lifelong and unbreakable cords of fealty and identity that family members possess for each other, and which even distance and alienation never quite erase, depend on this biological matrix. No other "family" form can replace it.

The radical equality, mutuality, and identity shared by family members are not mysterious or dreamily metaphysical. These are not metaphors. They are not symbolic ways of indicating the presence of emotional ties. The family matrix is as real as anything social scientists could measure, and much more sublime. It is no more subtle or beyond the state's concern than is the correct judgment that the factor of *equality* of marital friendship lies at, or very near, the heart of the state's legitimate judgment that polygamy is wrong and should not be lawful, even to the point of making criminal a person's attempts (indeed, rendering their acts merely *attempts*) at plural marriage. For anyone can see at a glance how, and how grievously, a polygamous "family" simply fails to be a family.

Anyone can see too that the morally compelling form of life described in this chapter is not one that two people of the same sex could establish. Anyone can see now why marriage is monogamous. Anyone can see why adultery is incompatible with marriage, especially but not only because adultery portends the possibility of illegitimate children. Anyone can see that, at least for any marriage that has borne the fruit of children, that marriage is permanent – that child embodies the couple's union and mutual self-giving, even after the couple divorces.

So far considered, then, placement with a same-sex "married" couple is a grave moral hazard to the child. If and when the child finally is exposed to the truth about marriage and sexual morality, he is much more likely to reject it, for accepting it would involve repudiating the relationship of those who have cared for him and loved him for years, if not decades. The child is then placed in the awful position of having to choose between filial devotion and adherence to the truth. It is a cruel choice – one that no child should be forced to make.

Conclusion

Obergefell put opponents of same-sex marriage on the defensive. Many Americans would go further. They would follow the Court's lead. After recognizing "decent and honorable" opposition, the majority added that, "when that sincere, personal opposition becomes enacted law and public policy, the necessary consequence is to put the imprimatur of the State itself on an exclusion that soon demeans or stigmatizes those whose own liberty is then denied." Justice Alito got it right: "By imposing its own views on the entire country, the majority facilitates the marginalization of the many Americans who have traditional ideas." "Today's decision ... will be used to vilify Americans who are unwilling to assent to the new orthodoxy. In the course of its opinion, the majority compares traditional marriage laws to laws that denied equal treatment for African-Americans and women. ... The implications of this analogy will be exploited by those who are determined to stamp out every vestige of dissent."

Defensive postures and pleas for tolerance of traditional notions will not stand up, certainly not for long, to this intolerant juggernaut. Only the courageous presentation of the truth and beauty of marriage and family stands a chance of staring down this specter haunting our society.

Chapter 6
The "Transgender" Challenge

Under what terms and conditions may adults require a twelve-year old boy, say, or a fourteen-year old girl – or *any* other minor – to strip naked in front of strangers?

At a time when keeping children safe from sexual exploitation has become an overriding social imperative, you might think that *there are no such terms and conditions!* You might think so especially because people go to prison now for having on their laptop just one picture of a naked child. This is the felony of possessing child pornography.

Now suppose that a minor is not only required to strip naked in front of strangers. Suppose further that the strangers are too. These strangers are *mostly* but not *all* other minors. A few young adults, high-school seniors who are eighteen or nineteen, are also present. Some of the minors do not look their age either: some girls and boys as young as fourteen have the bodies of grown women and men. Suppose for sure that *all* of these naked strangers are at or post-puberty. Finally, suppose that sundry other adults (teachers and coaches, say) come and go as they wish amidst this apparent debauchery.

Again, you might intuitively reply: *this just is not to be done!* After all, any adult who arranged a birthday-suit party for the neighborhood teens would face criminal charges for endangering the welfare of minors. Anyone who secretly viewed this get-together would be guilty of voyeurism (a crime in most states). A participating teen who snapped a cellphone picture of nude proceedings at the school gym would be suspended and probably expelled. If he or she texted the photo to even one friend – what is colloquially known as "sexting" – this child could be charged as a juvenile delinquent with transmitting child pornography.

Perhaps you have by now concluded that *no one* can lawfully require your child or teen to strip naked in such circumstances. No one could blame you if you did so conclude. But you would be quite wrong: the adults running your public-schools do this all the time – in bathrooms, before and after gym and swimming classes, in the athletic locker rooms, in the communal showers.

So, there *are* sufficient terms and conditions for adults to exercise this improbable, and fraught, power to require your children to strip naked in front of strangers.

What are these terms and conditions?

The essential moral safeguard, the *sine qua non,* the non-negotiable limiting condition for all this nudity is that it be disassociated from *sex,* that it not be *erotic,* that *the sexual gaze be excluded,* that *these minors not be the subject or object of sexual arousal.* School bathrooms, lockers, and showers must be maintained, as a matter of school policy and practice and culture, as *non-sexual* zones of nakedness.

This is accomplished in an essential way by limiting such facilities to persons of the *same sex.* This is the condition that makes requiring minors to strip in company morally permissible. It is the term which distinguishes all this nudity from the obscene. It protects school authorities from engaging in acts which would otherwise be akin to pimping.

This is the normative context in which to critically consider the exploding number of political fights and lawsuits over policies about gender dysphoric – or "transgender" – students' bathroom, shower, and locker room access in public schools. These crucial decisions are also made in private schools, as well as in other settings where people are more or less obliged to undress in front of others. But the leading "bathroom" disputes so far have been limited to public middle- and high-schools, and I shall discuss one of those cases here. As the Congregation for Catholic Education noted, in its 2019 document "Male and Female He Created Them," an "ideology" about "gender" "leads to educational programs and legislative enactments that promote a personal identity and emotional intimacy radically separated from the biological difference between male and female."

I

Consider the experience of some northern Illinois high-school girls, as it was described in federal court decision handed down in early 2019, in the case of *Students and Parents for Privacy v. High School District 211.* District Judge Jorge Alonso wrote that several high-school girls were "startled, shocked, embarrassed, and frightened by the presence of a male in the girls' restroom," most especially when "female student A" was "exposed to this male's penis."

Now you might well say: surely *this* is a violation of school rules, and maybe a criminal act.

This naked guy was no "streaker" or everyday pervert. He was a student. But the school did nothing to discipline him. The school authorities sent him there, under what they quite accurately called a "compelled affirmation" policy governing "transgendered" students' access to intimate school facilities. The results of the burgeoning litigation over this repudiation of the essential condition for requiring any kid to strip in a group have mostly been disappointing. These courts' reasoning – sometimes in support of "affirming" schools' policies and sometimes deployed to strike down policies which respect the essential condition – has been defective and sometimes irresponsible, even though the case for common sense and decency has been cogently made by able attorneys in numerous cases across the country.

These arguments are presaged for readers of this chapter by the name of the plaintiff group in the Illinois litigation: "Students and Parents for Privacy." These arguments are sound as far as they go. But by and large they have not been successful. These arguments could be, and should be, amended to connect more explicitly the plight of the "startled" and "shocked" girls with the truth about sexual arousal and modesty and chastity.

The case against "compelled affirmation" policies needs to be more explicitly and vividly *sexualized.* By that I mean that the argument against these policies must be rooted in the civil liberties of objecting students, as they pertain to the morality of acts which cause sexual arousal, which instigate impure thoughts, which threaten the healthy psycho-sexual development of young people, and most importantly in our cultural moment, the right not be forced to be the object of another's sexual gaze, the occasion for the arousal of another person. This improvement synthesizes the prevailing "privacy" contentions (again, sound so far as they go), and extends them and focuses the argument on something that even judges who have been mesmerized by "transgender"-affirming propaganda might find hard to sanction: opening intimate facilities to anyone of the opposite sex (understood as anyone bearing the sexually provocative body parts of the opposite-sex) imposes psycho-sexual trauma on countless non-consenting youths, and constitutes a form of sexual exploitation like those described in the vignettes with which this chapter opens.[1]

This amended argument is timely offered. The legal issues are yet unsettled. Although results in the cases so far have mostly been unfavorable to privacy-seeking girls and boys, there are just a few of them and the ideological tenor of the federal courts is changing for the better quite rapidly. The Supreme Court has not yet (as of late 2019) weighed in. Even though considerable cultural clout has been exerted by those who think that transgender affirmation is the next big step towards personal authenticity, many more see it for what it is: a rebellion against our created natures as embodied souls male and female, which is an indelible sexual identity inscribed in every one of the billions of cells in each of our bodies. Many rightly see, too, that the "transgender" political movement moves society closer to what Pope Benedict XVI called the "barren cult of the individual." In this transgender "moment" we are seeing, more perspicuously than ever before, what a social world determined by solipsistic individualism looks like. It is not a pretty sight.

II

Wait a minute. Someone might object: are not these "affirming" policies clearly illegal? Is it not true that Title IX – the federal law which bans sex-discrimination in any program receiving federal funds, and thus in any public school in the country as well – makes special provision for single-sex restrooms, locker rooms, and showers, as well as for "separate living facilities for different sexes"? Indeed, it does: this seminal federal sex-equality

---

1   I hasten to add that in this chapter I leave aside another compelling argument against "compelled affirmation" policies, namely, that they force upon a whole school community forced participation in a *lie*, for these policies require everyone to treat and speak of a *boy* as if he were in truth a *girl*, albeit one "trapped" in a boy's body.

law carves out safe harbors for sex-segregation in such intimate areas. Even the uber-progressive Justice Ruth Bader Ginsburg wrote in the Supreme Court decision admitting women to the theretofore all-male Virginia Military Institute, that under the Equal Protection Clause of the Constitution this college would have to make considerable adjustments to its rooming facilities, to protect the privacy of all students. The key federal civil rights statute as well as the Constitution are therefore both in line behind the "startled" girls' claim to privacy violated by "compelled affirmation" policies – so it surely seems.

Not exactly. These safe-harbor provisions are all *permissive*. They are not mandatory. Nowhere do the federal civil-rights laws say expressly that institutions receiving federal funds *must* maintain sex-segregated intimate facilities. These laws stake out an exception to what might otherwise be the relentless march of "sexual equality" all the way to co-ed showers. These permissions were claimed by all the secondary and elementary schools in the country until yesterday. And they should be mandatory: if the constitutional right of privacy means anything, it means that middle- and high-school principals cannot make children and teens strip naked in front of the opposite-sex. But they remain permissive. School districts and courts persuaded that girls who are "transgendered" are in fact boys, and which are persuaded further that there is no real harm to students scandalized in bathrooms and showers, are legally at liberty to command affirmation from everyone in the building.

How then have courts and school officials so "persuaded" themselves?

III

Some judges and school authorities pointedly note that this or that "transgendered" boy – in truth, a girl renamed "Ash" or "Gavin" – has enjoyed peaceable access to the male restroom for a while, because (they say) no one complained until the parents of a few prissy students organized opposition and filed a lawsuit. The only feature of this thought that possesses potential as a sound reason for choosing a policy is its implicit appeal to the justification of *consent*.

It will not do. For one thing, it is unfair to construe the absence of objections (if indeed that is the case) as consent. Even if consent may sometimes be given implicitly, silence does not invariably denote agreement and many students and parents may believe that they are not being asked to consent, or that they have the right to object. Or they may be afraid of being labeled haters or the like if they do object.

Besides, none of the minors is capable of *effective* legal consent. The whole complex of crimes around "child pornography" conclusively presumes that up to age eighteen anyone therein depicted – even if she and her parents signed consent forms in quadruplicate – is not capable of consent. If all the sophomores at the local high school decided to get together during study period and skinny-dip in the pool, these same school authorities would rush to stop the reverie. The ringleaders would be suspended, notwithstanding their plaintive cries that everyone was cool with it. No high-school principal boasts about how happy the varsity boys and girls basketball teams are – and let us say that they *are* happy – now that they shower together.

One school official enamored of "compelled affirmation" tried an end-run around consent. This official said that students who do not like sharing the restroom with the opposite-sex should just leave. This flip-of-the-hand is contemptible because it is contemptuous of students who care about modesty. And while some students might be able to run from high-school debauchery to a morally sane private school or to home-schooling, many cannot. For most people, anyway, geography and finances conspire to make the local public school a legally required rite of passage for their children.

The next rhetorical strategy of many judges and school officials is to deny that anyone's privacy is, as a matter of fact, compromised. According to these public authorities, the girls "frightened" by a penis in the restroom can – and should! – take refuge in a stall. Thus, the problems associated with common intimate spaces vanish by dictating that "communal" is now to be replaced by divisible personal private spaces within the same restroom. A Florida federal trial court judge described this alchemistic act. He wrote in *Adams v Saint John County Schools* (2018) that the school board "has a legitimate interest in protecting student privacy, which extends to bathrooms. Allowing transgender students to use the restrooms that match their gender identity does not affect the privacy protections already in place. When he goes into a restroom, Adams [the 'transgendered' student] enters a stall, closes the door, relieves himself, comes out of the stall, washes his hands, and leaves. Adams has encountered no problems using men's restrooms in public places."

Another federal judge, who went on to reject modest students' "privacy" claims, put the lie to all this talk about how private a school's common intimate facilities could be. He wrote that "[f]emale students changing for PE and sports are sometimes topless in locker rooms. Students changing for swimming are sometimes naked ... Many girls shower after swim class in open showers visible to other students in the locker room. [Swim class is mandatory for freshmen and sophomores.] Use of a bathroom stall for changing is not a good alternative, because such stalls are cramped and less sanitary than a locker room." Many schools make everyone shower after gym or before entering the pool.

The divisible-privacy argument is also blithely indifferent to peer pressure and the often-cruel social world of the teenager. Running to a stall when a boy named Sue comes in, and hiding there until Sue leaves, is a sure bet to court derision and even ostracism by more "enlightened" classmates, fortified in their errant beliefs by the school's own declaration in favor of "transgender" bathroom access. The same candid federal judge just noted recognized that the schools conveyed that those objecting to the penis were "bigoted and intolerant." Worse calumnies were lobbed in that case by other students.

Pro-transgender judges' indifference to the grim reality of teen intolerance is especially biased, for these same judges in these same opinions exhibit an exquisite solicitude for the slightest perceived slight of an Ash or a Gavin. These judges have held that as a matter of law Ash and Gavin should not be asked to do anything that they do not want to do for fear of feeling like they are somehow "different." For them, no risk of potential "stigma" too small; for everyone else, no sacrifice to make Ash and Gavin comfortable as members of the other sex is too great. Offered by a sympathetic but not unrelentingly "affirming" school the choice of using a single-occupant bathroom (instead of the toilets assigned to his or her true sex), refusing "transgendered" students have been backed up by courts, even when the only reason given is that this student would feel like others thought he or she was somehow different. Where are these "startled" girls to hide when they want to shower, or change for swimming class? The judges who glibly advise these girls to avert their eyes in the bathroom do not even allege that they could do the same in the locker room and the showers.

IV

These cases often turn as a technical legal matter upon whether the "transgender" student is a victim of "sex" discrimination. One branch of this way of thinking about "compelled affirmation" turns on the established recognized proposition that "sex discrimination" includes "sex stereotyping." In other words, someone cannot be fired for gender-nonconforming behavior; a boss cannot lawfully get rid of a woman because she wears no make-up or a man because he does. In the seminal Supreme Court case of *Price Waterhouse v Hopkins* the Justices wrote that the accounting firm could not lawfully condition the female plaintiff's promotion on such "stereotypical" factors as her ability to "walk more femininely, talk more femininely, wear make-up, have her hair styled, and wear jewelry." In one important lower court case a male plaintiff was discriminated against for "carrying a serving tray too gracefully [and] taking too active a role in child-rearing."

It is unclear, though, in which way this chain of thought supports "compelled affirmation." In these cases school officials who resist "affirmation" take the position that *no* boy can behave so effeminately, and *no* girl can be such a rabid tomboy, as to get himself or herself sent to the bathroom of the opposite-sex. The message to a "transgender" student who is really female is the same: act as much like a guy as you wish and you still have to shower with the girls. The same message is sent to a boy who earnestly believes that he is a she. Whatever the shortcomings of this way of thinking, "sex-stereotype" discrimination is not among them.

The reply might be: but Ash and Gavin are *really* boys. But they are discriminated against on the basis of sex (or sex-stereotyping) because they are sent to the girls' restroom. Again, I do not see it. I see that on this construal the school has decided to treat two "boys" differently, one "cisgender" and the other "transgender." But this is not a case of discrimination on the basis of "sex." It is discrimination on an adjectival basis *within* the one sex, as if the distinction were between little boys and big boys, or between kids from the trailer park and those from the showier part of town, or maybe between smart and dumb boys. Or to take a page from history: making black boys shower separate from white boys was surely unjust discrimination – on the basis of race, not sex!

The most creative attempt to weave a sex-discrimination case out of these facts – or, perhaps, to throw a cloud of confusion over them – belongs to Judge Anne Williams, of the Seventh Circuit Court of Appeals. Someone unfamiliar with legal analyses might think that these cases are about contending definitions of "sex": is it determined by "biology" (is it "natal"), or is it more "experiential" where someone claims to be "transgender." Judge Williams does not agree. She would explode the view that biological "sex" is binary! After expressly treating separately the case of ambiguous genitalia and thus of "intersex" babies, Williams wrote: "[I]t is unclear that the sex marker on a birth certificate can even be used as a true proxy for an individual's biological sex. The marker does not take into account an individual's chromosomal makeup, which is also a key component of one's biological sex. Therefore, one's birth certificate could reflect a male sex, while the individual's chromosomal makeup reflects another."

There is no scientific doubt (notwithstanding some legal confusion) that no more than a tiny fraction of children is born with "complete androgen insensitivity." These babies have XY (male) chromosomes but also female genitalia. These babies are however female. And the vast majority of babies are born with unambiguous male – or female – DNA and with corresponding male – or female – genitalia.

V

In judicial reasoning about "transgender" access, there is an ambient appeal to the very exceptional nature of an Ash or a Gavin. These judges say in so many words: what is the big deal about just one kid who will be a quick in and out anyway? But it is not just one. Yes, individual plaintiffs appear in each of the lawsuits so far considered. But plausible estimates of the number of self-identified transgender students in some high schools across the country range up to nine percent. There is a further reason to expect that, as "compelled affirmation" policies and the wider elite-cultural promotion of transgender identity proliferate, so too will the number of confused high-school students. Copy-cat sexual identity "questioning" is already a documented phenomenon.

Besides, the numbers do not matter in one crucial way. The "don't worry it is just one kid" reply presumes that the good end in view is quantifiable and divisible. It is not. The good end which stands behind and explains sex-segregation policies like the ones we are discussing consists of the serenity and security born of the presence of a no-exceptions, categorical rule, backed up by earnest enforcement: *no* boys in the girls' restroom. Period. It is a good effectively subverted where it is the case instead that, at the door to the girls' showers, the sign says: "Ordinarily there are only girls present inside, and there are never a lot of boys. You can be sure that you will not see, and be seen by, no more than a couple of naked men. Have a good day." Would anyone seriously suggest that it would not matter if, for example, only boys who promised not to stay long were admitted to the girls' showers? Or that boys are generally not permitted in the girls' lockers, save for the captain of the football team and his best friend? Or that the boy's basketball team shares changing rooms with the girls' team, but only during home games.

I think not.

There is another more important sense in which a valuable good is indivisibly, and universally, at stake. Even if there is one Ash or Gavin in the building, wherever school officials by into "affirmation" and make it school policy that the whole community do so too, *every* student's understanding of himself or herself as an embodied soul, make or female in body and mind, is gravely threatened. Even if there is one "transgender" student, so long as the school promote "affirmation," then each student's self-understanding as such an integrated unity is contradicted. The reason is that, if anyone's true sexual self is "trapped" in the wrong body, anyone's could be. If anyone's could be, then everyone possesses a "gender identity" which might be different than his or her natal sex. Everyone is then trapped in a world of body-self dualism.

VI

The next justification for "compelled affirmation" on offer is also about privacy. But this time the reasoning is prescriptive, not descriptive. It is morally evaluative, not a claim about whether *in fact* anyone's privacy is compromised. Now it is about "startled" or "embarrassed" students' *legitimate* expectations of privacy, and what exactly constitutes a *wrongful* intrusion thereon.

Judge Anne Williams wrote that the Kenosha, Wisconsin, schools (which resisted "compelled affirmation") believed that "transgendered" Ash's "mere presence would invade the privacy rights of his *male* classmates." Well no, it is not only about anyone's "mere presence." We will shortly see that, although introducing the male gaze into a girls' bathroom (or the female gaze into the male facility) *is* a serious harm, the harm is also that sooner rather than later a man's bare genitals will be conspicuously "present." The judge who decided *Parents for Privacy v Dallas School District No. 2* (which is by the way in Oregon, not Texas) identified both these harms, when he said that the offended students do not want to "see or be seen by someone of the opposite biological sex while either are [sic] undressing or performing bodily functions in a restroom, shower, or locker room."

True. But so far stated we are stuck in the emotive sands of what some people happen to *want*. The frightened students assert that they have a right to "be free from government-enforced, unconsented risk of exposure to the opposite-sex when they or members of the opposite-sex are partially or fully unclothed." Indeed, they do. But *why?* What is the solid morally compelling ground of this putative right?

Here is where the good arguments so far adduced against "compelled affirmation" reach the limit of their effectiveness. They have so far been reticent to expose themselves (speaking for the moment of the arguments as if they are persons) to rebuttal for their depending upon controversial claims about sexual morality, about the immorality of sexual arousal in these contexts, and of chastity more generally.

Let me explain.

Remember that Judge Alonso described the girls' reaction to an exposed male in their restroom as "startled, shocked, embarrassed, and frightened." This is typical of the descriptions in the "transgender" cases. It is typical of what the law generally calls "emotional distress," which is a matter of adverse emotional and psychological experience, of feelings of repugnance. These feelings are not legally inert; one can successfully plead for and recover damages for the unjustified infliction of "emotional distress" in some circumstances, usually involving what is by any standard of decorum or decency someone else's "outrageous" conduct.

But these feelings do not count for much in our law. They count for very little when they are provoked by someone else's exercise of their constitutional rights, such as free speech. They have not counted for much at all when a judge in the grip of progressive sexual ideology, informed by medical professionals that it is a matter of life-or-death by suicide for Ashton or Gavin, come to the equities of frightened teen-age girls. These judges think that it is the girls' reaction which is unjustified, if not outrageous.

Simply put, that some high-school girls are upset is not a very strong legal argument. Stacked against Gavin's or Ash's basic mental health if not their survival (because "suicidal ideation" is a regular feature of the psychological account of the "transgendered" protagonist in these cases), the firecracker has in fact proved to be a dud. And there is a genuine weakness here, or one might rather say a true limitation, in the argument so far mounted against "compelled affirmation." The girls' reaction could be described exactly the same way as Judge Alonso described it if, say, they walked in and saw a female classmate doing something in the common area which really should be done in the privacy of a stall. In that scenario, the girls would understandably be disgusted, and offended, and "shocked." But that would be the limit of the harm to them: their dissonant feelings are quite unpleasant and should not have been occasioned by their female classmate's breach of decorum. Or, and it is a bit impish to put it this way, their reaction in the real case ("startled, shocked, embarrassed") could well describe their reaction if instead they walked into the bathroom and saw a ... *zebra,* sitting there in the middle of the bathroom. Whether the zebra is male or female or confused about that does not affect my point. I presume the zebra was naked.

There is thus a *sliver* of legal truth (if you will) in Judge Williams' otherwise reckless assertion: "[t]he School District has failed to provide *any* evidence of how the preliminary injunction will harm it, or *any* of its students or parents. The harms identified by the School District are all speculative and based upon conjecture, whereas the harms to Ash are well documented and supported by the record."

On this way of arguing the issue out, there is a conflict between the transient unpleasant feelings of a few teens over against the basic well-being and possibly survival of a suffering classmate. This is not a promising argument way to win the case for modesty. The argument has to be recast, strengthened. Reason more compelling that the intuitions and feelings of some students need to be introduced. Judges who would rule in favor of the next Gavin or Ash must be made to see that, in order to do so, they must adopt reasons that even they would say prove way too much.

A holding in favor of the next Gavin and Ash must be shown to be a holding against sex-segregated intimate facilities. The amended argument is a stark appeal to moral norms of sexual purity: young people whose sexual urgings are newly stirring and yet to be fully comprehended and mastered, should not be forced by public authorities to strip naked with strangers where the circumstances include exposure of, and to, members of the opposite sex. To do so is make young people the objects of others' sexual arousal, and to tempt them into sexual arousal. Doing so is unfair to all of the students and threatens to harm them by impeding their attempts to develop chaste habits. Doing so would be morally akin to requiring high-school students to sit together and watch stag movies every week. The increased vividness accompanying real-time exposure is more tempting, and the persisting connections to those whom one has encountered naked make the temptations more apt to be acted upon.

Once these specifically sexual harms are identified, spoken, and moved into analytical view, it is easy to see then that the "transgender" student is in no way made the object of discrimination – unless one makes the gratuitous assumption that he or she is same-sex attracted. In other words, a teenage girl who believes that she is male should be assumed to be sexually attracted (still) to males, so that putting her in the boys' restroom is a disservice to *her* attempts to be chaste. The DSM V, for example, does not list same-sex attraction among the eight clinical indicators of gender dysphoria.

No judge has yet been put to this test.

Yes, Judge Williams in the *Kenosha* case observed that "a transgender student's presence in the restroom provides no more of a risk to other student's privacy rights than the presence of an overly curious student of the same biological sex who decides to sneak glances at his or her classmates performing bodily functions." I do not know what this means for women. For guys, it refers to the chap at the next urinal who seems, well, to be a bit nosy. But this sort of "curiosity" is not necessarily, and usually is not, voyeuristic or sexual at all. Sometimes, to paraphrase Freud, "curiosity" is just curiosity, especially when we are talking about kids whose own bodies are undergoing changes which naturally make them wonder, a bit, about how they are doing *vis-a-vis* their peers. In any event there are social norms and informal sanctions available to restore proper moral order in the restroom, precisely because it is understood by one and all present that such "gazing" is inappropriate, and creepy.

I should like to add this addendum, from the more strictly legal analytical point of view: one very welcome effect of *sexualizing* the argument along the lines I trace is that it becomes quite certain that an "androgen insensitive" baby, when she grows up, is a girl for the relevant purpose of moral and legal analysis. Even if some would argue that XY chromosomes make you a boy, albeit one with discordant genitalia, any debate about "sex" is settled here as elsewhere to the *relevant* meaning or aspect of it; *namely, those parts of the body which, unclothed and in our culture, are the sites of sexual arousal, titillation, tension.* This is standard variety legal analysis of usage and meaning, even Aristotelian in its approach to specifying the meaning of terms where they pertain to purposeful human activity.[2]

VII

Someone might object: does reliance upon the revised argument described in these pages – that the key has to do with forestalling sexual temptation and unwanted gazing – imply or entail that homosexual or lesbian teens must be somehow identified, and excluded from the restroom, shower, and locker of their biological sex? Is it to be a "witch hunt" for homosexual and lesbian teens? Is it smart to introduce into the mix of premises contested norms of sexual morality? In other words, does my argument founder on the shoals of dread "heteronormativity"?

The answer is no. For one thing, a humane and loving response to this challenge would include counseling any same-sex attracted boy or girl to consider more private options for intimate activities than the often-crowded

---

2   I should like to add too that a full response to the "transgender" movement must include a refutation of the whole notion that "compelled affirmation" is actually helpful or good for Ash or Gavin. See Appendix Two for that refutation.

lockers or bathrooms. It is no service to the moral or psycho-sexual health of such a boy or girl to habitually place them among naked persons who sexually arouse him or her. This is not to pick out same-sex attracted people for particular scorn. It would be very perilous for any heterosexual high-school boy to be given the option of showering with the girls' basketball team.

A second reason: the presence of a same-sex attracted person in the locker room or toilet is not nearly the breach of faith – and the threat to others' peace of mind – that the presence of a naked member of the opposite sex would be. For one thing, the latter would be unmistakable and the former might well not be "out," so that no one other than the "closeted" young man or woman would even *know* that there is a breach of the non-arousal protocol. But even where someone is "out" and known to be same-sex attracted, there is a vast asymmetry between that prospect and that of a transgendered member of the opposite-sex, namely, that while both may be equally sources of inappropriate sexual gazing, only the latter presents not the jarring presence of unwelcome male (or female) sex organs, and in that a temptation to sexual arousal for everyone else present.

A frank hetero-descriptivity does, however, underwrite the argument proposed here: the vast majority of people, including teens, are sexually aroused by nude members of the opposite sex, more keenly when they are pubescent and fit as are most high-school students.

Third. *Any* purposeful sexual gaze in school showers, lockers, and bathrooms is inappropriate, should be discouraged, and should be eliminated insofar as it reasonably can be. This prohibition should be vigorously enforced, not as a measure of disapproval of same-sex attraction or of teens suffering from gender dysphoria, but for the sake of the one norm of sexual conduct which the position here defended surely does depend upon: that if the state is going to make my daughter or son strip naked in front of strangers at school they better damn well make sure it is not for the sexual pleasure of the other kids.

Conclusion

The 2019 Vatican document on gender theory states, "In all such [gender] theories, from the most moderate to the most radical, there is agreement that one's gender ends up being viewed as more important than being of male or female sex, ...The effect of this move is chiefly to create a cultural and ideological revolution driven by relativism, and secondarily a juridical revolution, since such beliefs claim specific rights for the individual and across society."

It is as if the Vatican writers were watching an American legal news channel.

Chapter 7
Foundations of Sex Equality:
A Comparison of Catholic Teaching
and American Constitutional Law

Introduction

Over the last few decades a very widespread consensus has congealed in American society in support of a thoroughgoing practical equality between men and women. By "practical" equality I mean equal pay for equal work, non-discrimination in the political and economic realms, the same civil and legal rights, equal access to higher education and all the other basic opportunities that people have, in a given time and place, to develop their talents and to pursue their callings – and, simply, to flourish as human persons. This hugely important *practical* equality is now taken for granted; it is no longer itself a subject of serious political or moral debate. And correctly so.

But there is much beyond and below this important consensus that is nonetheless quite troubled. "Beyond" it lies a nest of crucially important practices and institutions of our common life, where radical reform agendas are promoted as an implication or as a natural extension of women's practical equality with men, or as a necessary presupposition of it. The whole nest of issues called women's "reproductive rights" is perhaps the most important example. Today anyone who opposes unlimited legal access to abortion or who objects to paying for other persons' abortifacient "contraceptives" courts being charged with "waging war on women." Phrased less belligerently by then President Obama thirty-nine years to the day after *Roe v. Wade*: "As we remember this historic anniversary, we must also continue our efforts to ensure that our daughters have the same rights, freedoms, and opportunities as our sons to fulfill their dreams."

Still other important matters, such as same-sex "marriage" and treating gender dysphoric children as if they are members of the opposite sex, are implicated, too. For they are often justified on grounds that include the norm against discrimination on the basis of "sex," a norm the roots of which remain in the notion that men and women are to be treated equally.

It seems that what, at a glance, appears to be an untroubled consensus that men and women deserve equal opportunity is really the fulcrum of fierce social debate, a contest of ideas fraught with potentially devastating consequences for human rights and human flourishing. It is important therefore the validity, not of the basic consensus itself, but of these (and other) extensions of the norm in favor of "sex equality." Doing that necessitates drilling down into its foundations. "Beneath" the operating consensus lies, as a matter of fact, a roiling and unsatisfying argument about the philosophical premises of equality between the sexes.

My exploration of these foundations shall take the form of a dialectical examination of attempts by two venerable institutions over the last generation to supply those foundations. These institutions have been concerned to explain and to justify, in a deep but nonetheless operationally consequential manner, the fundamental equality of men and woman. One of these institutions is the United States Supreme Court. The other is the Catholic Church. This chapter compares the *foundations* of the equality of men and women put on offer by these two institutions. My aims are to evaluate each on its own terms, and to see if the two accounts can be brought into fruitful contact. I conclude that *both* the civil law and the Church's position suffer from an unfortunate hesitation to locate the equal dignity and worth of men and women upon *reasonable* grounds; that is, in metaphysics and in a sound theory of moral value.

Mulieris dignitatem ("*MD*") is a sound *theological* treatise but, as such, it is not well-adapted for effective use in civil society debates about the meaning and scope of sex equality. The civil law is too superficial, too glib, and simply *un*reasonable at key points. The most compelling foundation for treating men and woman as equals is, of course, their shared human nature. But it is an essential part of explaining what that means to grasp our shared "human nature" by identifying the basic components of human flourishing which men and women share in equal measure, and in which they have an equal interest. Moral truth available to unaided reason is the soundest foundation of sex equality, at least after one accepts that male and female are metaphysically (and beneath that, biologically) similarly members of the human race. The Church can and should articulate and defend it in season and out of season, alongside complementary theological considerations.

I

Since the early 1970s the Supreme Court has authoritatively interpreted the Constitution to ban sex discrimination. In sum, the Court has held that the Equal Protection Clause of the Fourteenth Amendment prohibits public authorities large and small (from the United States itself all the way down to the most remote local school district) from treating the sexes differently. Any law or regulation which derogates from this equal-treatment rule is presumed to be unconstitutional. It may only be rescued if it serves especially important government interests in a very circumspect way.

Without exception the Court's sex equality cases reject any putative justification for a challenged law which sounds in "stereotypical" notions about women's proper place – in the home, or anywhere else. All attempts to support even broad, defeasible cultural presumptions about male or female roles are effectively forbidden. Thus, the terms "parent" and "caregiver" are replacing "mother" and "father," while "spouse" increasingly effaces "husband" and "wife." And now that practically all military occupations are open to women, there is probably no frontier left for the sex egalitarians to conquer; while eliminating vestiges of sex discrimination on the ground and all across the economy remains a work in progress, it is already the case that *legally* such discrimination is almost wrong. The results of this equality initiative have been far-reaching. But what is the basis for it?

Wholesale critics of the Court's sex equality jurisprudence are few. Many observers disagree with this or that specific holding. But not many take a crack at it root-and-branch. One who did was the late Justice Antonin Scalia. He maintained in an interview with Berkeley Law Professor Calvin Massey that the sex-equality jurisprudence was ill-founded. Scalia maintained that the Constitution does not prohibit such discrimination, but neither does the Constitution *require* it. Scalia concluded legislators today are free to write as many or as few sex-neutral laws as they wish. But there is no basis in a sound approach to interpreting the Fourteenth Amendment

for holding sex non-discrimination is unconstitutional. Justice Scalia's brac-
ing criticism was primarily based upon his reading of what the Americans
who enacted the Amendment in 1868 had in mind. "Sorry to tell you that,"
he added, but "[n]obody ever thought that's what it meant."

II

The social developments and rising consciousness which produced the sex-
equality revolution in constitutional law reverberated in the Church, albeit
to less effect. The Church's solemn teachings that the ordained priesthood
is forever reserved to men and the exceptionless wrongfulness of contraception and abortion have so far held firm. Even so, it is anyone's guess
precisely how widespread is the practice of contraception among Catholics,
and how high the incidence of abortion and support for female deacons and
priests is among them. But these levels are surely disturbingly high. The
Church's resolve to hold tight the truth on these matters has not made its
pastors insensitive to the criticism that the Church retards women's
progress in the world and that its teachings simply do not accord with the
human dignity of half the human race.

Partly as a conscious response to these criticisms, Pope Saint John Paul
II in 1988 promulgated an encyclical letter on the dignity and vocation of
women – *Mulieris dignitatem*. Its central claim is that men and women are
"essentially equal." The vast bulk of the letter is given over to account of
how and why that is so. In *MD* the Pope also consciously sought to bring
his largely theological reflections into fruitful contact with the sex equality
then being established in the civil law of most countries, including the
United States.

Pope Saint John Paul II organized his reflections in *MD* into what he
called a "meditation" on women's "dignity and vocation" [*MD* 18]. It is an
altogether theological "meditation." What I mean is that the equality of
men and women is itself largely a *theological* concept: *MD* identifies (and
explains and defends) the "essential equality" of men and women by virtue
of their similar – if not identical – relationships to the Creator and to the
Lord Jesus, as well as by the coincidence of their paths to salvation.

Thus, in *MD:* "Everything that has been said so far about Christ's attitude to women confirms and clarifies, in the Holy Spirit, the truth about

the equality of man and woman. One must speak of an essential 'equality,' since both of them – the woman as much as the man – are created in the image and likeness of God" [*MD* 18]. "*Man is a person, man and woman equally so,* since both were created in the image and likeness of the personal God" [*MD* 6; emphasis in original]. Man and woman are "equally capable" of understanding and receiving the Christian faith, "of receiving the outpouring of divine truth and love in the Holy Spirit. Both receive his salvific and sanctifying 'visits'" [*MD* 20]. There is the one Spirit, the one Baptism, the one Gospel for all humankind: "[T]he evangelical idea is addressed to human beings without any distinction of sex" [*MD* 25]. "The dignity and vocation of women – as well as those of men – find their eternal source in the heart of God" [*MD* 18]. "It is a question of understanding the reason for and the consequences of the Creator's decision that the human being should always and only exist as a woman or a man" [*MD* 2].

MD is quite remarkable among post-Vatican II papal teachings for its scant references to theological writers, to the Church's philosophical tradition, and to other papal writings. The sources relied upon by the Pope in *MD* are predominantly Scriptural. *MD* is largely a profound *biblical* "meditation" on the dignity and vocation of women, even a Scripture-based *apologetic*. Big chunks of the document are devoted to showing that biblical texts which appear to sanction (or even to command) women's subordination to men, do not do so when properly contextualized and interpreted. The Pope interprets Saint Paul's assertion that the husband is "head" of the family, for instance, as a call (or command), not for wives' subordination to their mates, but to *mutual* self-sacrifice, each spouse to the other. It is a matter of "*mutual subjection out of reverence for Christ*" [*MD* 29; emphasis in original].

The Pope in *MD* also develops lengthy explanations of other biblical stories; among them are the creation of woman from Adam's Rib; Eve as the temptress of Adam; Jesus's choice to make only men Apostles – to rebut the notion that Christianity sanctions discrimination against women. This is centrally what I mean when I say that *MD* is an "apologetic": it seeks to rebut certain arguments against the faith and to remove a certain impediment to accepting the faith, namely, that the faith entails injustice towards women.

The heart of this biblical apologetic is the example of Jesus. "In all of Jesus's teaching, as well as in his behavior, one can find nothing which reflects the discrimination against women prevalent in his day" [*MD* 16]. Christ opposed the "tradition which discriminated against women," a tradition "in which the male 'dominated' without having proper regard for woman and her dignity"; Christ's "whole attitude towards women" was "extraordinary, if seen against the background of his time"; "It is universally admitted – even by people with a critical attitude towards the Christian message – that *in the eyes of his contemporaries Christ became a promoter of women's true dignity* and of the *vocation* corresponding to this dignity" [*MD* 15; emphasis in original]. "*Christ's way of acting, the Gospel of his words and deeds*, is a consistent *protest* against whatever offends the dignity of women" [*MD* 18; emphasis in original].

III

The biblical texts upon which John Paul II relied in *MD* – *Genesis*, chiefly – and the common religious sense of the average American reveal what human observation and reflection both show: what makes human persons unique among and superior to the earth's other creatures – and what supports the conclusion that humankind may rightly "dominate" the other creatures of the visible world" – is shared *equally* by men and women. They all possess a rational nature – the capacities for conceptual thought, self-awareness through time, and free choice. Combined with two indubitable additional premises – that men and women alike each possess an individuated body and distinctively human genetic material – one can conclude that men and women are indeed *essentially* equal, for they are (male and female alike) equally and wholly human persons.

Our civil society's discussion about the foundations of legal equality has lately been impoverished by its emancipation from Biblical foundations. The new canonical story which American law now tells about its foundations is quite different from the one the founders told – and from the one most Americans still would tell. Now the general rule of constitutional law (which I do not suggest is enforced scrupulously, or even well understood by those who favor it) is that no law may rest upon a "religious" basis. Now the source or alleged ground of "equality" today – at least in respectable public discussion – cannot be our common origins (as per *Genesis),* or our common supernatural destiny or our common life in Jesus.

What *have* been the asserted deep roots of the dramatic movement in American law towards equal rights for women? Legislative achievements favoring equality of the sexes owe most immediately to concentrated political power, not to philosophical argument. Philosophical questions can be and often are sidestepped so long as an unproblematic measure of comparison is at hand – such as the legal rights and privileges of white men. A legal ideal or goal of non-discrimination can take the place of attaining genuine and true equality.

But courts are not like legislatures in that judges (and Justices) are obliged to give a systematic explanation for their rulings, and that explanation must in some decisive way arise from or within the Constitution. The obvious candidate for this role is the constitutional text which declares that "all persons" are entitled to the "equal protection of the laws." At the level of political theory, one could also try to mine some positive sources – societal consensus, the "democratic way of life," "evolving standards of decency," norms "implicit in the concept of ordered liberty" – to support legal claims. (Note that the sources just indicated in quotes are common fare in the judicial opinions about equality of rights over the last two generations.) But our courts and leading legal theorists have not made much of this opportunity, for the simple reason that the equalizing decisions beginning in around 1970 were an abrupt break with legal tradition and past social mores.

The Supreme Court has instead relied greatly upon shopworn appeals to the prejudices of the enlightened classes. The recurring story line in the key case holdings is that only the misogynistic "stereotypes" of benighted legislators could possibly explain a challenged law establishing some distinction based upon sex. As the proffered (or imagined) rationale is one beneath any decent person's credit, the Court's conclusion goes through without further serious effort.

Here is a longer account of what I mean. In the 1992 *Casey* decision (which affirmed the central holding of *Roe v. Wade)* the three authors of what they called a "joint opinion" (and they were Republican appointees Kennedy, Souter, and O'Connor) wrote that "not so long ago" a concurring opinion of the Court affirmed the common-law principle that a married woman had no legal personality independent from her husband, who was regarded as her head and representative in the social state. The *Casey* Court possessed an odd sense of timing; they quoted from an 1873 case as if its holding and the society of which it spoke were still extant.

The Court's habit has been, in other words, to *back into* invalidating sex-sensitive laws. The Justices have launched no cogent theory of equality. Instead they have traveled the *via negativa,* holding in case after case that the challenged lacked altogether a basis in reason. The Court was sometimes wrong; even sex-discriminatory laws which were struck down possessed *some* basis in reason and experience. The Justices nonetheless said that the challenged law owed entirely to some outdated, biased view of women's place.

The issue in *United States v. Dege* (decided by the Supreme Court in 1960) was whether a husband and wife could form a "conspiracy" within the meaning of a statute, which had been enacted in 1948, making it a crime for "two persons" to combine for criminal purposes. The Court's majority scoffed at the allegedly "medieval" view that "husband and wife 'are esteemed but as one person in law.'" These Justices eschewed what they described as "blind imitation of the past." Insofar as they allowed that some reason of substance underlay the view pressed unsuccessfully upon them, they saw but two grounds: joint responsibility would either "make for marital disharmony, or that a wife must be presumed to act under the coercive influence of her husband and, therefore, cannot be a willing participant." Dispatching these two reasons was quick work. The former was "unnourished by sense; the latter implies a view of American womanhood offensive to the ethos of our society." In other words, justifying an equalizing decision today is little more challenging or complex than flicking aside the benighted, dead hand of the past.

The dissenting Justices in *Dege* asserted that the case could not be decided by application of "breezy aphorism[s]." No such "simplistic approach" as the majority's would do. "It is not necessary to be welded to fictions," or to unenlightened views on "women's suffrage or capacity to sue," to nonetheless hold that the risk of conspiracy prosecution ought not to be permitted to threaten the "confidentiality of the marriage relationship." Conceding as they ought to have that those married are two, not one, these Justices maintained that a "wife, simply by virtue of the intimate life she shared with her husband, might easily perform acts that would technically be sufficient to involve her in a criminal conspiracy with him, but which might be far removed from the arm's-length agreement typical of that crime." It was partly the risk of substantive injustice that undergirded the statutory exception. Besides: "the concept of the 'oneness' of a married couple may reflect an abiding belief that the communion between husband and wife is such that their actions are not always to be regarded by the criminal law as if there were no marriage."

When the Supreme Court approved an automatic exemption from jury service for women in 1961, to cite another example of the *via negativa*, it involved a law which said that only women who registered their desire to serve were placed on the jury list. The Court accepted the state's rationale that a "woman is still regarded as the center of home and family life." Louisiana repeated the argument in the 1975 case in which the Court struck down the automatic exemptions ("to regulate and provide stability to the state's own idea of family life"). The Court there struck it down precisely as an inaccurate generalization.

The Court did not in these or in any other of its cases directly engage any normative question about women and the home. They instead recited statistics showing that (roughly) half of all women were employed outside the home, saying: "While these statistics perhaps speak more to the evolving nature of the structure of the family unit, they certainly put to rest the suggestion that all women should be exempt from jury service based solely on their sex and presumed role in the home." The Court recognized that an exemption was convenient and productive for some women, but that it is "untenable to suggest these days that it would be a special hardship for each and every woman to perform jury service or that society cannot spare any woman from her present duties." "[M]any" women may fall into this category, and the Court recognized that it could be "burdensome" to administratively sort them out. But the state did so for men who could show hardship or that their service to the community could not be interrupted. "[A]nd the administrative convenience in dealing with women as a class is insufficient justification for diluting the quality of community judgment represented by the jury in criminal trials."

The most common analysis to which laws differentiating male and female responsibilities have succumbed is this: never denying but always weakening the force of any statistical generalization about the different choices or tasks of men and women, the Court lowers the boom on the "stereotypical" generalization. In 1992 the Court could say that the view of women as the "center of home and family life" is "no longer consistent with our understanding of the family, the individual, or the Constitution." Perhaps so. So far, though, this descriptive generalization is insufficient to support a normative conclusion that an allegedly outdated law is unjust.

IV

The central affirmation of *MD* is that men and women are *essentially* equal. That conclusion standing alone does not engage the issues of equal treatment which preoccupy the civil law of gender discrimination today. The truth that men and women are "essentially equal" (in an unrestricted sense, without limitation to divine things or to the matter viewed in relation to Jesus) does not establish anything that is – or was – really in doubt. So the Pauline texts assert *both* that "[t]here is no longer Jew or Greek, there is no longer slave or free, there is no longer male or female: for all of you are one in Christ Jesus" [*Gal.* 3:28], *and* "wives be subject to your husbands, as to the Lord, for the husband is the head of the wife" [*Eph.* 5:22-23].

Sepulveda conceded, in his great disputation with de las Casas about what justice required of Spaniards in the New World, the American-Indians' essential equality with Spaniards. But Sepulveda nonetheless asserted that enslaving and making war upon them could be *morally justified,* due to their barbaric practices and also by what we could describe as their possession of radically inferior gifts. America's antebellum slaveholders did not justify slavery on metaphysical grounds. Few of them credited any religious (or other) account of separate origins for the white and dark races. Slavery was instead justified on less ambitious grounds, such as the contingent fact that those who were enslaved were not developed enough to make good use of freedom or that emancipation could be socially ruinous. Slaveholders could and many did affirm the "essential" equality of slaves as children of the same God for whom Jesus died. The slaveholders nonetheless thought of grounds upon which to rationalize their denial of any *practical* equality to slaves.

The conclusion defended in *MD* is not incompatible with affirming, for example, that women are not men's equal in many of life's endeavors. The conclusion in *MD* is not incompatible with one traditional ground for gender discrimination, namely, that although women possess a rational nature and flourish in the enjoyment of the same basic human goods as do men, women as a group are in fact more governed by passion than they are by reason or, at least, they are more governed by passion (as a group) than are men (as a group). That women were almost invariably less physically powerful than men further persuaded men (and some women) that the male was the natural protector of the female.

Pope Saint John Paul II established contact with the law's concerns when he referred several times to "traditions" of "unjust discrimination" and to "situations in which the woman remains disadvantaged or discriminated against by the fact of being a woman." But this "tradition" is never described. The Pope in *MD* supplies no examples of "unjust discrimination." No cause or explanation for any (unspecified) discriminatory practice is stated, much less defended as a cause, save (to some extent) that they are the product of original sin [*see MD* 8].

MD's oblique obscure manner of identifying injustices against women is matched, unfortunately, by an equally brisk and uninformative comparison to "significant changes of our times" [*MD* 34]. John Paul II welcomes "the hour" "when the vocation of woman is being acknowledged in its fullness, the hour in which women acquire in the world an influence, an effect and a power never hitherto achieved." At this time the "human race is undergoing a profound transformation" in its understanding of woman's contributions to the improvement of humanity's condition. But the Pope does not further describe or analyze these changes; the contrast between an outmoded and justly abandoned "tradition" and a new dawn of justice is drawn, but is nowhere described, explained, or judged in more subtle terms. This ellipsis is one of the great weaknesses of *MD*.

V

MD makes almost no contact with the Church's own social doctrines, including one of its leading claims about social justice: that society make sure that workers receive a "family wage," or an effective substitute therefore. Where a "family wage" policy (or an effective substitute) is in place, a healthy relationship between family life and remunerative employment can be enjoyed, a relationship which allows for women (mainly, as a matter of fact) to remain at home with children.

It might have been more productive of constructive (that is, critical) engagement with the civil law if *MD* had taken a more subtle and, even, a slightly more favorable view of "tradition." The Pope could have attributed some of the discriminations in law and custom between men and women found in history and in some societies today to circumstances of labor, personal security, and the dangers and difficulties of childbirth and child-rearing which called for a significant (though not all-encompassing) division between male and female spheres. In developed societies until quite recently, many legally recognized distinctions between male and female were not dishonorable, insofar as they were efforts to establish and maintain the family as the basic – or as a basic – unit in society, functioning in the economy and in political or legal affairs through its head, which was invariably assumed to be the husband.

These discriminations were no doubt infected with some degree of unjust and uncharitable attitudes towards women. Surely by some point in the last century these practices became so ham-handed and out-of-sync with custom and mores as to become – in a word – unjust. Almost all economic opportunities in the developed world today are equally suited to women as well as to men. The gifts of women and men in almost all non-familial undertakings are so comparable (if not equal), that discrimination against women in pay and other aspects of employment and participation is unjust. The family is not what it used to be. Today, even if one recognizes the continuing value of treating the family as a basic social unit, there is no persuasive case for re-introducing the laws discarded in the recent past.

The Pope could have avoided any implicit endorsement of these discarded laws and still put him himself in a position to address the central question in law and life today for women, namely, how a society by and through law can arrange things so that women can integrate career and motherhood *without* sacrificing the equality of women and men. But as far as I can see in *MD*, he did not. Though the Pope in *MD* discusses profitably the vocation of women to marriage and motherhood, and the importance of esteeming and using her gifts of "femininity," he does not attempt to integrate these insights with his approval and recommendation of the removal of any barriers to women's career advancement.

VI

We saw earlier in this chapter how the Supreme Court's gender equality cases were boosted into orbit by generalizations which were a mix of normative and descriptive. In other words, the Court (and our law more generally) moved toward women's *practical* equality by a non-moral evaluative route: certain legal categories and standards which (by hypothesis) were meant to be mere accommodations of women's preferences or *de facto* needs or convenience were out-of-sync with the contemporary world.

The Court has moved the "tipping" point at which a roughly accurate generalization inevitably moves from being a helpful (and lawful) accommodation in light of most women's choices and situations, to an "outmoded stereotype," and thus a denial of equal rights for women. Leaving aside all questions about to what extent it is either a constitutional or judicial matter, this movement is, I think, basically sound. Not only Christian faith but decent human living requires both men and women to make commitments to use their gifts in serving others and to carry out those commitments faithfully. Law, public programs, and social practices should support both men and women in doing that. And doing *that* amounts to eliminating almost all discrimination against women in the workplace, in politics, in public service, in education and the like, for almost all such opportunities depend upon gifts possessed in abundance and in roughly equal proportions by men and women.

The relevant organizing principle of the civil law is that being female should not compromise or even affect a woman's free and equal personhood. This commitment includes but transcends the aspiration of early feminists that the difference between man and woman become legally as inconsequential as that between black and white, a goal very nearly complete. But the Court has reserved to itself no resources for dealing with the central question about women in civil society today, which is how to integrate career and motherhood *without* resorting to immoral means of "controlling" one's reproductive life. On the contrary, the *Casey* Court asserted that "for two decades of economic and social developments, people have organized intimate relationships and made choices that define their views of themselves and their places in society, in reliance on the availability of abortion in the event that contraception should fail. The ability of women to participate equally in the economic and social life of the Nation has been facilitated by their ability to control their reproductive lives."

VII

Notwithstanding the considerable attention that the Church's pastors have given since Vatican II to the needs of modern women, they have yet to say anything of significant value to women about a characteristic, and characteristically life-determining, question: how many children should a specific woman have? It is more than fifty years since *Humanae vitae* taught that couples have a serious moral responsibility to conscientiously decide, on the basis of "serious" reasons, about spacing children and even to postpone pregnancy for an indefinite time. But nothing authoritative and of consequence has been said since 1968 about those "reasons," or about the factors pertinent to choosing when to engage in the marital act, and about the number of children which the parents' vocations call for.

One reason for this silence is that the whole subject of birth control is taboo in almost every American parish. So it is too in most Catholic spiritual writing. This is sadly ironic: our pastors have all-too-often decided not to disturb the laity about contraception out of a misplaced respect for our consciences. Our pastors deprive faithful Catholics of preaching and teaching about what almost all of us most desperately need, which are the tools with which to figure out what Jesus wants from us when it comes to having children. The laity are thus abandoned to the untender mercies of American culture. The vast majority of American Catholics have the same number of kids as the vast majority of Americans.

Even in the beautiful meditation on the vocation of woman which is one subject of this chapter, Pope John Paul II did not take up this question about how Catholic couples should go about discerning the number of children they should seek to have. Nor did he say anything in particular in *MD* about how women are to meld family and career. Catholics should be thankful for the development of a rich theology of woman and of motherhood since Vatican II. Much has been written from the Catholic perspective about the dignity of women. Some has been written about being a Catholic wife. But we have nothing comparable for the lay man; that is, for husbands and for dads.

The Church has been dead silent on the meaning of the Pauline concept of "headship" in the family. In my judgment, this gap owes not only to general neglect. It owes substantially to anxiety about the Church's *credibility* to speak to masculinity and manhood after the sexual abuse crisis (with its revelations about an alarming prevalence of homosexuality in the priesthood). Much of the Church's unfortunate silence about men owes, though, to defensiveness about the preservation of the priesthood to men, to the Church's alleged sexism – to the existence of what some deride as the "patriarchy."

There is nonetheless a desperate need for more than a theology of the body and a serious theological treatment of women and their dignity equal to that of men. Each of these was supplied by Pope Saint John Paul II. There is a crying need for a theology of *men,* of *masculinity,* a distinctively *male* complement to *MD.* It might reasonably enough have been thought in decades and centuries past that men could take care of themselves and that the political as well as theological challenge was to somehow bring women into a standing equal to men's standing – whatever that was. But the days of men's nonchalant dominance of politics and business and education are numbered. Already at least the lay man is nearly rudderless when it comes to how to understand himself as a Christian father to his children, a Christian husband to his wife, and a Christina man faced out to the corrupted secular world all around him.

VIII

Another promising ground for affirming women's essential equality with men has also been evacuated from most discussion in the law: human nature. Here I mean to supplement what I said earlier about the *metaphysical* identity of the sexes about how all possess a rational nature, that all are embodied spirits and so on. This human nature is metaphysical, too, in the sense that it is about permanent objective aspects of what it means to be a human being. I speak now of human flourishing as an aspect or expression of human nature. For we can know a being's nature by its capacities, and its capacities by its acts. We know human act by their objects: the basic goods at which human beings aim and seek to achieve by their sundry purposeful choices. Call this the "human perfection" ground and meaning of equality.

Men and women are equal by virtue of the truth that for everyone everywhere since Adam and Eve, knowledge, life itself, friendship with fellows and with God, marriage: these are *good*. They are all basic aspects of human flourishing. Precisely the categorical and universal quality of these basic goods grounds the exceptionless moral norms that anchor basic human rights (as we have seen throughout this book, starting in the Introduction). This whole complex of ideas about value, moral absolutes, and objective moral truths is absent from our civil law too. We retain much of the discourse of human rights, to be sure. It is a discourse without feet.

Conclusion

Most Americans affirm the essential equality of men and women on grounds very much like those adduced by Pope John Paul II in *MD*. If one sampled Americans at random and asked them: "what makes people equal, one to the others," the most common answer would be something like: "because we are all God's children," or "we are all brothers and sisters in the Lord." This is not only true. It is sufficient for each of us to hold as we go about daily business. Both our Church and our political society, however, face perplexing questions about the meaning of being male and female, about how the sexes differ and how they are the same, and what justice requires when it comes to matters where treating men and women at least a bit differently seems right. Facing these challenges squarely and honestly requires more than what suffices in everyday operations. The *moral* equality of men and women – the truth that they are perfected all the same by participating in the same basic human goods – is a resource scarcely brought to bear so far upon these important questions.

Chapter 8

The Future of America's Catholic Institutional Ministries

In his "Cardinal's Column" for February 26, 2012, Francis George, then Cardinal Archbishop of Chicago, offered this bit of advice to his Chicagoland readers: "If you haven't already purchased the Archdiocesan Directory for 2012, I would suggest you get one as a souvenir. On page L - 3 there is a complete list of Catholic hospitals and healthcare institutions in Cook and Lake counties .... Two Lents from now, unless something changes, that page will be blank."

Cardinal George was not prophesying a global ink shortage. He was not predicting a printers' strike. He was forecasting one effect of the federal Department of Health and Human Services "contraception" mandate, which went into effect on August 1, 2013, and which was fully enforced against religious employers starting one year later. Cardinal George issued a warning, not a threat. He was not telling the Obama Administration (whose "mandate" it was) how the Church would respond if the mandate is not rescinded, the way a mother might tell her child: "[I]f you touch the pot on the stove I will take away your Gameboy." It was more like: "[I]f you touch the hot pot you will burn your hand."

Cardinal George articulated, that is, an *intrinsic consequence* of the mandate, given what it requires and what being a Catholic institutional ministry requires. He declared that the mandate will "make it impossible for Catholic institutions to follow their conscience." He added that this "[in]voluntary sacrifice" involved not only hospitals, but the Church's "universities and many of her social service organizations."

It did not work out as grimly as Cardinal George feared. "Two Lents" later there are still many Catholic institutional ministries listed in the

Archdiocesan Directory. The acute phase of the specter of mass institutional martyrdom passed when the Trump Administration in 2017 began to relax the mandate's strictures. These relief efforts have themselves become enmeshed in litigation across the country, just as was the original mandate. A large number of religious employers subject to the mandate gained indispensable relief. The Supreme Court upheld this relief in the *Hobby Lobby* and *Zubik* cases.

The net effect of all that the Trump Administration has done for the sake of religious liberty as it bears upon Catholic institutions has been great and good. But the underlying cultural and, to a lesser extent, legal drift remains ominous (as the preceding chapters so strongly suggest). The forces which produced the HHS mandate have been blunted by the Trump ascendancy. They have not been dissipated. These forces are centrally the "liberty" of self-definition and its corollary "identity" politics. They will resume their march through the remnants of America's Christian culture no later than when the Democrats next control the Executive Branch.

In this chapter I shall explain why the future of Catholic institutional ministries *as we have known them* is bleak. I shall also explain why the prospects for new forms of institutional witness – more modest and nimble than those which have come before, but in some ways more robust – are bright.

I

Cardinal George was no saber-rattler, no Chicken Little: the sky really was falling, or very nearly so. The HHS mandate did not quite make it "impossible," though, for Catholic institutions to follow their consciences. As the Cardinal made clear later in his column, the mandate unjustly put Catholic institutions to the test. There is always a morally upright option available for choice. It is always possible to act conscientiously. It is just that the only possible option may be to bear an injustice, to suffer, even unto martyrdom. From Saint Paul through to John Paul, the Christian way has been populated by countless saints and martyrs who cleaved to the Pauline injunctions "do not do evil that good may come of it," and "it is better to suffer injustice than to commit it." "Do not be deceived: neither the immoral, nor idolaters, nor adulterers, nor sexual perverts, nor thieves, nor the greedy, nor drunkards, nor revilers, nor robbers will inherit the Kingdom of God" [1 Cor. 6: 9-10]. In other words, it is never "impossible" to be faithful. It is just that martyrdom could possibly be the consequence. And Cardinal George was speaking frankly about institutional martyrdom.

The HHS mandate presented the threat of martyrdom because it effectively exploited the huge asymmetry in Christian moral life indicated by Saint Paul and by John Paul II, namely, that all the good which one has done or which a Catholic organization might yet do, does not justify or excuse choosing to do what is exceptionlessly morally wrong. "What does it profit a man, to gain the whole world and forfeit his life?" [Mk 8:36]. The "masters of the world" include those who run Catholic apostolates, including bishops who run them.

To anyone who might wonder about sacrificing the Archdiocese's hospitals for a moral truth which America's Catholics violate and which their bishops usually ignore – I am speaking of the truth expressed in *Humane vitae* – one should reply that the issue of the HHS mandate was not just contraception. Or, rather, it was "contraception," which was stipulated by law to include abortifacients. The line between contraception – an intrinsic evil which admittedly involves no injustice – and the grave injustice of abortion is blurred not only in law and in FDA-sanctioned "science." These evils run together in culture, in popular thought, belief, action. Pope John Paul II wrote in *The Gospel of Life* of "the close connection which exists in mentality between the practice of contraception and that of abortion is becoming increasingly obvious." They are "fruits of the same tree," he continued. "[I]n many instances [they are] rooted in a hedonistic mentality unwilling to accept responsibility in matters of sexuality." Both "imply a self-centered concept of freedom, which regards procreation as an obstacle to self-fulfillment." This fusion of moral horizon about sex is "demonstrated," the Pope concluded, "by the development of chemical products and intrauterine devices which really act as abortifacients" [13].

Cardinal George was surely not glib about institutional martyrdom. Nor was he keen to embrace it. He knew too that the matters to which witness is being given must be proclaimed as *truths*, and not as (merely) parochial "can't helps" or tribal customs or distinguishing characteristics of one's religious community. Notwithstanding Robert Bolt's depiction of him as an existential hero dying for his very *self*, Thomas More accepted martyrdom for the sake of witnessing to the truth about marriage and about Christ's Church. (Recall our discussion of Bolt's existentialist More in Chapter Two.) In *Veritatis splendor* Pope John Paul II described "martyrdom" as an "affirmation of the inviolability of the moral order, [which] bears splendid witness both to the holiness of God and to the inviolability of the personal dignity of man" [92]. The Church should not sacrifice its hospitals for the sake of its own "identity," for a group totem, or for a disciplinary rule. But every Catholic must be prepared to sacrifice all, if the alternative is faithlessness.

Cardinal George was right: Catholics must steer clear of support for contraception or abortion, and perhaps most especially of the "mentality" that the mandate mandates. Catholics must bear faithful witness against both of these evils, and against the "mentality" which links and legitimizes them. This moral duty is more acute for a Catholic institutional ministry than it is for each of us, more strict even than it is even for Catholics collaborating under another banner, such as a secular business which strives to live up to Catholic social justice principles.

II

Catholic charities, hospitals, and universities bear the name "Catholic," which no diocesan bishop should permit any outfit to do, save where they – the institutions – have undertaken to corporately inhabit and communicate the Catholic faith. Canon law and sundry Church documents impose this vigilance upon the bishop as a duty. Every Catholic is bound by baptism to announce Christ to the world. But when Catholics collaborate in some work and would publicly identify that work *as* Catholic, its Catholic character must be more vivid, more true, unequivocal, unsullied, than what individual Catholics may tolerate. Catholic institutional ministries must bear especially perspicuous witness, in word and deed, to Christ's revelation of God's truth and love, so that nonbelievers might be led to faith, and the already convinced may be strengthened and encouraged in the Christian life.

The difference between the Catholic Worker House, for example, and a municipal homeless shelter lay not in the quality of the hospitality on offer, or in the greater good cheer with which they deliver it. There is no reason to suppose that one is characteristically superior to the other on either of these metrics; after all, the city might well be able to afford firmer mattresses than the Worker House and, notwithstanding a partially deserved reputation for bureaucratic callousness and sclerosis, many government social workers are very dedicated people. The difference is that Dorothy Day did corporal works of mercy; that is, she provided a bed and a meal to people in order to show Christ to them, and in order to see Christ in them. Mother Teresa and her collaborators performed menial tasks in their hospices, jobs which Americans typically receive about eight dollars an hour to do. The Missionaries of Charity do far more than those underpaid orderlies do. What they do is priceless.

New York's CYO director in the 1930s, Rev. Edward Roberts Moore, expressed the complex character of Catholic charity well enough: "[F]or us Catholics, program without *apostolate* is a contradiction in terms. ... We must always keep first things first: neither more participants nor swelling biceps in themselves mean stronger character, better citizens, or whiter souls."

Another way to grasp the difference might be to reflect upon why it is that priests and consecrated religious do not fight our country's wars or hold our nation's public offices. Their recusal does not owe to the immorality of public or military service. It owes rather to their particular vocations, which involve chiefly bearing unequivocal witness to the Kingdom. This vocation excludes involvement in acts that others, including Catholics, not only may perform but often should perform.

It is not a matter of two moralities, one for the holy and another one for the bingo-players and rosary-prayers. It is a matter of different vocational responsibilities. Jesus's vocation was incompatible with him marrying and having children. But there is nothing wrong with matrimony. Catholic institutional ministries have a specific and important vocation, which carries with it special, and higher (if you like), moral responsibilities. There are things which they must not do which other upright Catholics may do. Practically speaking, a Catholic institutional ministry must steer clear of material cooperation with evil which individuals or those running a secular organization could in conscience accept.

For anyone to kill the unborn is a grave injustice. For any doctor to kill an unborn child is worse, for a doctor's vocation is to heal and never to harm. For a *Catholic* hospital to involve itself in killing the unborn is even worse. It is not only an injustice and a betrayal of the Hippocratic Oath. It bears false witness to the true faith. It is a lie about God and the Kingdom. It blocks people from coming to understand and thus to accept the truth about Jesus Christ, and undermines (to some extent) the efforts of those who do bear true and faithful witness.

A Catholic ministry must always bear acute witness to moral truth, and never lead people to act immorally. Keeping the commandments is necessary, but not sufficient. For it needs to be remembered that, in transmitting the Gospel, word and witness of life go together. Witness by itself is not enough, because even the finest witness will prove ineffective in the long run, if it is not explained and justified by what Saint Peter called "giving a reason for the hope that is in you". 1 Pet 3:15.

A Catholic institutional ministry needs, then, a double immunity, or twin free spaces: first, to conform all its "deeds" to the demands of morality; second, to "proclaim" the Word of the Lord." For no one can read off of any Christian's best good works truths accessible only to faith, such as the possibility of preparing material now for the Kingdom. Carrying on a vibrant institutional witness allows those who experience a Catholic ministry to see the path of moral righteousness (which John Paul II in *Veritatis splendor* said is the way of salvation for those who faultlessly fail to profess Catholic faith). Explaining such a perspicuous witness permits those who come near to encounter a living vision of the meeting place of heaven and earth.

III

The HHS mandate was an unprecedented. Never before had the United States martyred a Catholic institutional ministry over a moral issue. Apart from recent martyrdom of Catholic family services (in Massachusetts, Illinois, Philadelphia, the District of Columbia and a few other places) over same-sex couples' adoptions, no public authority at any level of government in America – federal, state, or local – has martyred an institutional ministry over a moral matter. This is a remarkable fact, given the sharp discord over sexual morality and life issues which has grown up over the last half-century. It is more remarkable in light of the anti-Catholicism that has permeated American history. This fact is remarkable testimony to the basic soundness of America's constitutional protections of religious liberty.

The infamous "Blaine Amendments" enacted in a couple dozen states after the Civil War characteristically cut off public *funding* to all "sectarian" institutions. They were principally aimed at Catholic entities and that is probably where they had their major effect. But these enactments (which were typically not statutes but state constitutional provisions) extended to non-Catholic denominational institutions as well. Except for Catholic elementary schools, these laws were not the sharp spear point of a weapon aimed at eliminating Catholic (or other "sectarian") hospitals, charities, orphanages, and reformatories.

This is not to suggest that these "Blaine Amendments" were benign – except perhaps comparatively so. There was in the late nineteenth century a developing conviction among many non-Catholic Americans that the doctrinal distinctions which marked the different Protestant sects simply did not matter much theologically. There was an accompanying conviction that they did not matter at all to the right conduct of political life. There was a good-faith belief that an effort to "separate" "church" from "state" in the specific sense of making a pan-Protestant Christianity the state's partner for services would well serve the common good. The negative implication for Catholic institutions was this: unabashedly Protestant state-assisted institutions – orphanages, Indian missions schools, most other public schools, some hospitals – escaped censure because, as most non-Catholics saw things, they were not "sectarian" but "religious" or perhaps "biblical."

Catholic *schools* were different, partly because *schools* were different. At least from the introduction of free public "common" schools starting around 1830 in the northeastern United States, these institutions were always closely associated, in purpose and character, with inculcating in students from diverse ethnic and religious backgrounds a common ethos, character, and understanding of American political life. They were engines of assimilation. Non-Catholics fervently maintained that Catholics most especially needed to attend what one historian described as these "culture factories."

The stubbornness with which Catholics insisted upon their rights to have their own schools and to some sort of public support for them keenly rankled, because these claims were – to most non-Catholics – confirmation that the Church's so largely foreign-born members "commanded" by a foreign "prince" (the Pope) harbored dual loyalties. Not only was public funding of these incubators of parochialism a non-starter. Even before the Civil

War, and more or less continuously until recently, there has been very significant opposition to the *existence* of Catholic schools. One prominent and not-distant example is the demonstrated attitude of a Supreme Court during the 1970s. In case after case the Supreme Court struck down states' efforts to funnel some public funds to what were mainly inner-city Catholic schools financially devastated by the exodus of wealthier parishioners to the suburbs, and by the skyrocketing costs associated with the disappearance of sisters who taught devotedly and nearly for free. The Justices were unmoved by the argument that without such assistance these schools would all close. The results in those cases rested upon doctrinal gerrymandering, suited to the result desired. And the reasons which the Court majorities gave for turning a deaf ear bristled with hostility to Catholic schools.

Eliminating public funds did little to slow the explosive growth of the Catholic institutions, which became pillars of the sub-culture which preserved the faith of America's working class population of Catholics for a hundred years. This stubborn, massive Catholic edifice of mediating institutions, occupying public space but wholly outside government control, called into being a whole body of church-state law about institutional ministries. These institutions and that body of law cemented a fruitful civil partnership between church and state, each working in its own way for the common good.

Entire congregations of Catholic sisters came into being precisely with specific ministries in mind (chiefly, healthcare and education). Indeed, the whole history of Catholic parochial education and of Catholic charities in the United States is rooted in aversion to parallel public institutions which were more or less openly Protestant. Viewed over the span of a couple generations, institutional ministries rooted in religious and, to a lesser extent, ethnic identity have been engines of assimilation into the wider mainstream of American culture.

IV

The Church's ministries have come and gone through the course of the Church's pilgrimage in America. But they have done so without being martyred. The rule is that Americans' recurring hostility to Catholicism has perennially expressed itself, politically and legally, in fights over public funding of, not over existential threats to, Catholic institutional ministries.

America's first hospitals were nothing like today's acute care facilities. Then, there was no "acute" care to be had. Hospitals at their inception were basically nursing homes for the ill and dying, a cross between our hospices and our long-term nursing facilities. Catholic hospitals first came to be when existing institutions were inhospitable to patients' Catholic faith. For example, up to the twentieth century even many "public" hospitals made it difficult for priests to administer last rites. Many Catholic hospitals were founded when Catholics could generally walk or be carried to a neighborhood Catholic facility, which they would choose for its spiritual comforts as much or more than for its creature comforts.

The number of Catholic hospitals has steadily declined over the last few decades, as these original animating purposes have faded. In 1922 between 15 and 20 thousand sisters were working in U.S. and Canadian hospitals. Now one could spend a month in a Catholic hospital and not encounter a professed religious woman. In 1930 there were dozens of Catholic hospitals in New York City. Now there is none. Saint Vincent's in Manhattan was the first to open its doors in 1849, and the last to turn off the lights, in 2010. The Catholic medical school is nearly extinct.

The forces behind all these developments are the stuff of business school seminars and of Washington policy briefings. The causes include relentless market pressures towards consolidation and thus towards partnerships with secular healthcare providers. These forces also include Catholics' current disinterest in specifically Catholic hospitals. Catholics go where other Americans go when they are ill, which is to the hospital covered by their health insurance plan. This consumer pattern owes, in turn, partly to the wholesale relocation of illness, suffering, and death from (mainly) the religious realm to the medical-scientific domain of cause and effect. Almost no one chooses a hospital now according to its, or one's, religious identity.

Fewer than one-third of the 194 Catholic colleges founded in the U.S. before 1900 survived into the 1950s. There are about 220 of them now listed in the Kenedy Directory. Many Catholic colleges came into being as places for the sponsoring religious orders to educate their own novices or seminarians. This was especially the pattern for women's colleges, as religious superiors undertook to educate legions of teaching Sisters. From the late nineteenth to the mid-twentieth century, local bishops typically did not permit Sisters to attend non-Catholic institutions and discouraged and occasionally forbade men to do so. Even in 1940, one of every five graduates of Catholic women's colleges was a nun at graduation, a proportion that did not decline until the collapse of vocations in the 1960s. Lay Catholics were often admitted to these colleges initially to help pay the bills. Those purposes are all gone now.

The total volume of Catholic Charities services is greater than it has ever been. But the *what* – as opposed to the *how many* – of it would be unrecognizable to anyone who dozed off during the Depression. Catholic Charities is now basically a government contractor; more than 60 per cent of its total budget comes from the state. The vast network of institutionalized childcare our deep sleeper knew is long gone. It was built to take care of those kids whose parents had faltered or, in a few cases, died. It was built when alternative care-givers, including "public" institutions and services, were indifferent or hostile to preserving in children the Catholic faith of their parents.

All those Catholic foundling hospitals and orphanages and industrial schools of yore have been replaced by a few homes for pregnant girls, by outdoors counseling, and by adoption and foster placement services.

This long-term institutional ebb and flow has included many cases of attrition by obsolescence and by market forces, where neither anti-Catholicism nor moral "impossibility" was involved. Whole tranches of institutional ministries have disappeared because their missions – and their clientele – did. Think of orphanages (which were always populated overwhelmingly by children with at least one living parent), and of "industrial schools" (think "reformatory). Think too of those many women's colleges which were finishing schools for the daughters of lace-curtain Irish, and other middle-class Catholic, families. Think finally of "homes for troubled girls."

These institutional ministries have all vanished. There is now scarcely an orphaned minor in this healthy country of ours. Today's reformatories are all run by the state; we call them "juvenile justice centers." Nobody's daughters are "finished" anymore. There are still places where pregnant young women can find refuge. But girls today do not go there for the reason that girls used to go there, which was to avoid bringing shame upon themselves and their families.

Government regulations enacted to standardize and to professionalize practices in medicine, education, and social services contributed to the demise of many Catholic institutions. This regime took an especially heavy toll on the Sisters' devoted but, perhaps, amateurish care for infants and children. Since the 1960s no Church university, hospital, or social service could survive without government grants or subsidized patronage (Medicaid, guaranteed student loans, and the like). These dollars have come with strings attached, a bargain which has contributed further to diminished evangelical zeal. Now, many Catholic institutions use their need for state money as an excuse for their compromised missions.

The increasingly non-Catholic clients (patients, students) of the Church's ministries would not necessarily diminish institutional Catholic character. Far from it. In our day, they do.

Misunderstandings of the meaning of "individual autonomy" and of "respect for conscience and of the imperatives of "pluralism" conspire to make these non-Catholic "consumers" into institutional stakeholders. More than a few judges and commentators have said that Catholic institutions resisting the mandate on religious liberty grounds violate the religious liberty of their employees. These observers say that those who run these places would "impose" archaic moral norms upon those who disagree with them.

Battered by the market and other social forces beyond anyone's immediate control, the institutions we have inherited suffer from mission fatigue, struggle to stay open, and all-too-often cannot find, much less hire, enough faithful Catholics to sustain a vibrant ministry. Of the Sisters' hospitals ca. 1921 Fr. Richard McCormick wrote: "There is a spirit, a soul, an atmosphere and ideal of service in the sisters' hospitals which they create and maintain and give their lives' best efforts to foster." In other words, any genuine Catholic institutional ministry *must* have a vibrant Catholic culture within it.

V

The Sisters of the nineteenth century asked: who will take care of our sick? They answered: we will. The American bishops of that time sized up state schools which sought to wean Catholic children of the faith of their fathers. They responded by building the largest private school system the world has ever known. They did it with the widow's mite. Catholics in all stations of life wondered who would keep the Protestant child-catchers at bay. They stepped up and built a vast protectory system.

It is no insult to the sacrifices and the fidelity of those heroic Catholics to say that their great works came into being, and were sustained for up to a century, for contingent reasons which no longer exist. Their achievement is no less admirable because their works were spared existential threats (like the HHS mandate) by contingent circumstances, too. Notwithstanding an ambient anti-Catholicism, theirs was a society which cherished religion, which believed in Providence and judgment and hell, which valued genuine devotion to Jesus Christ, and which maintained, in both law and culture, Biblical morality about killing, sex, and the family.

This is not our world.

It is no insult to our forbears to observe that their institutions were kept on a Catholic course by other contingencies which no longer obtain. I mention a few of those internal course stabilizers: the fact that almost all Catholic institutional ministries were sponsored by consecrated religious; the specifically religious – indeed, salvific – aims which as a matter of fact animated these good works (those who put shoulder to wheel worked to save their souls and the souls of those they helped); the huge free space in civil society, room unoccupied by government and professional licensing and guild regulations; the shared experience of Catholics as a disfavored minority, an identity which was reinforced by the hierarchy's disciplinary rules against collaborating with non-Catholics in religious and charitable works, rules which Leo XIII reinforced in *Longinqua,* his 1895 encyclical letter on Catholicism in the United States.

Those sponsoring congregations are gone now. The government is everywhere. Vatican II encouraged precisely those collaborations which Leo discouraged. America's Catholics are almost all universalists now. The dwindling number of Sisters are no exception. The vibrant Catholic sub-culture which all those contingent factors brought into being, and which sustained institutional ministries for over a century, is gone.

In *Gaudium et spes* 42 the Council Fathers wrote that "when circumstances of time and place produce the need, [the Church] can and indeed should initiate activities on behalf of all men, especially those designed for the needy, such as works of mercy and similar undertakings." Almost all of the "circumstances" relevant to the foundation of today's tripartite ministry (in health, education, charity) have changed. It would be a miraculous co-incidence, then, if the past of Catholic institutional ministries were con-scientiously judged to be the right blueprint for the future.

Nostalgia for a "golden age" of American Catholicism will not do. "Back to the future" it shall not be. America's Catholics will henceforth have to follow the core example of their nineteenth-century forbears. Catholics today are called, not to stubbornly maintain ministries which no longer witness to the Gospel, but to found new ones which will.

V

Then Father (later Cardinal) Avery Dulles wrote decades ago: "No one doubts that health, education, and welfare are good and necessary things. That is not by itself a reason why the Church ought to do them. Otherwise, the Church would have to grow vegetables, maintain a police force, and manufacture clothes. The Church is not called to do everything good but only to do those good things that fall within its divinely given mission."

Fr. Dulles here implied what Vatican II (in *Gaudium et spes*) explicitly affirmed: Christ "gave His Church no proper mission in the political, eco-nomic or social order." The Church's mission is religious. It is divinely given. This declaration in *GS* not only means what it most often is thought to mean, which is that the Church belongs to no political party and that it has no portfolio of plans for political affairs. It means also what Fr. Dulles indicated: even the good works which the Church performs in the private sector (if you will) do not reflect a "social" or "economic" agenda. They are *part* of the Church's religious agenda, which is the only agenda it has.

Christians should always be keen to care for society's downtrodden and marginal. They should (as *GS* said) seek opportunities in prevailing "circum-stances' to perform good works. The reasons why they should do so have nothing to do with any prevailing egalitarian political theory. They have noth-ing to do with feeling better about oneself. Christians do good works because the Christian life is love in action. Meeting others' needs is how Christians manifest the truth that, in Christ, we are all brothers and sisters.

The deepest principles behind yesteryear's institutional ministries are thus non-contingent. Those principles were – are – a burning conviction to live out the Gospel command to *do* the Father's will, especially (but not only) as it pertains to the neediest among us. In doing so Christians do what Jesus asks them to do, which is to announce – bring, proclaim, manifest – Him to those we serve. Witnessing to the truth is the surest way for Christians to do social justice. As the Fathers of Vatican II said in the Constitution on Divine Revelation (*Dei Verbum):* we hand on the message of salvation "so that by hearing [it] the whole world may believe, that by believing it may hope, and that by hoping it may love." A world which loves will be a world overflowing with good works.

The question about the future of Catholic institutional ministries is thus not about whether, but about *how,* to live out these timeless convictions. The issue at hand is, in what way can we make these principles concrete, today, here.

VI

If we inspect the signs of the times as our forebears did and as Vatican II says we must, we will discover that the institutional ministries of tomorrow will be large in number, but each smaller than those presently listed in the Kenedy Directory. The institutional ministries which we should build will deal much more with the spiritually poor among us than with the physically ill or hungry. The hungry and the poor shall perhaps forever be among us. Christians are always called to serve them. But our government considers itself obliged to do so too, and the government is a jealous competitor in these fields. That is one reason why the ministries we have face martyrdom.

Tomorrow's ministries will be found at the interstices of social structures, operate para-professionally, and rely more upon volunteers and contractors than a regular workforce. They will have to keep a low-profile, and in some cases operate off the grid. Institutional ministries henceforth must be strategically chosen so as to make particularly prudent use of our scarce material and human resources. We do not have fifteen or twenty thousand Sisters on hand. These forthcoming ministries will be more evangelical than the preservationist institutions of old, if only because America's Catholics need to be re-evangelized. Catholic institutional ministries in the future will almost all be lay-initiated and lay-managed. The Vatican Council stated in the "Decree on the Apostolate of the laity" that the "*apostolate* in the social milieu, that is, the effort to infuse a Christian spirit into the mentality, customs, laws, and structures of the community in which one lives, is so much the duty and responsibility of the laity that it can never be performed properly by others. In this area the laity can exercise the *apostolate* of like toward like. It is here that they complement the testimony of life with the testimony of the word" [13].

Today's mega-ministries – the hospitals, universities, and charitable networks – are so intertwined with a hostile intolerant host culture and law that their abiding "Catholic" aspiration is, really, no more than to avoid undeniable participation in grave injustice, or at least to keep their number to a minimum consistent with staying in business. They have lost their prophetic value. They do not bear clear and consistent witness to the truth. Many do not try.

The prognosis for today's mega-institutional ministries is grim. We already see, if only through a glass, darkly, that the half-billion dollar hospital, the research university, and publicly subsidized Catholic Charities cannot be sustained as genuine Catholic *apostolates*. Tomorrow belongs to the smaller, leaner ministries already at hand (like the Catholic Worker House, Saint Vincent dePaul, and hospice), and to those which faithful Catholics call into being.

VII

In the gathering gloom we can see some promising, concrete pathways for a springtime of institutional ministries. These ways fall into two main groups. One is comprised of modified versions or recognizable adaptations of today's institutional ministries. The other marks out pressing needs and objective, where the shape of an institutionalized response must be drawn up.

In healthcare the future of Catholic care lies, first, in expanded hospice work. For it is there that the spiritual realities which should, and once did, suffuse the art of healing still come to the fore. In addition, various bands of doctors, dentists, nurses, and other medical professionals could organize a week or more of "shock treatment" for underserved populations, especially among immigrants. The venue could be a "pop-up" storefront or a mobile treatment center. It is also past time for a distinctively Catholic "Doctors Without Borders" to be founded.

In social services, the future lies with services to immigrants, prisoners, parolees, and other very marginal social groups. At the level of public policy, Catholics should work with others of goodwill to make and maintain just immigration and criminal laws. All persons should do what they can to see to it that the just laws are fairly enforced. At this level there is no room for a specifically Catholic institutionally ministry. With regard to undocumented immigrants, small Catholic institutional ministries could and should meet legitimate material needs which no one will meet and do so even at the margins of legality. But perhaps the most distinctive service which such a ministry could perform is to ameliorate the *moral* hazards of living outside the law. These people are consigned practically to lives of secrecy and deception. Their lot is peculiarly prone to treating others unfairly, such as when an undocumented person with neither license nor insurance causes a fatal auto accident. No cure for these temptations and ills is within the gift of any Church group. But Catholics would better witness to their Savior's love for migrants if they ceased conspiring with them to deceive the authorities, and instead did all that they can do to make migrants lives upright.

Those who are imprisoned, those diverted from prison, and those recently released from state's custody constitute a promising field of institutional ministry. It is true that the state hovers nearby, and that is a caution signal. As a matter of fact, however, our society is presently most unforgiving of our offenders. They can scarcely find a place in the modern economy; their communities of origin are usually morally chaotic; and almost nobody else cares very about these folks.

Perhaps the most distinctive contribution a Catholic institutional ministry could make in this area is to act always with a view to requiring a proper moral responsibility in all persons ministered to, for the tendency among the relatively few others who are willing is to excuse or explain away the depredations of offenders, to treat criminals as if they are the *victims*.

I treat the future of Catholic higher education separately, in the next chapter.

Turning now to a couple of areas of great need, where organizational vehicles and mission refinement would be needed, the first area is in the area human procreation. Government, market, and cultural powers are conspiring to indoctrinate our young people, especially young women, into grossly immoral practices and the mentality which rationalizes them. One challenge to any institutional remedy is that the most morally freighted areas of medicine are undergoing ideological purification. Headlines about pharmacists and Plan B, about the American Psychological Association and its disapproval reparative therapies for same-sex attraction, and about compulsory abortion training in medical schools, all illustrate this point. Most recently, the state of California made it illegal to administer any therapy to any minor – even with parental consent – Intended to change one's same-sex attractions. In addition, our country's increasingly centralized methods of service delivery and payment – think of Obamacare and the HHS mandate – make it difficult to engage in a Catholic ministry, if it is to be a source of a professional's full-time remunerative employment.

The Catholic inroad here may be gained by thinking of systematized free or pay-as-you-go services, provided off-the-grid by healthcare professionals whose livelihoods are secured elsewhere. The need extends from soup-to-nuts; that is, from morally upright birth control all the way to proper post-natal care. Perhaps the most urgent need here is that which calls for the most distinctively Catholic response. The "Catholic" value-added in this neighborhood of issues is usually limited to instigating compliance with the moral law; natural family planning is the crown jewel value.

An institutionalized response to this crisis would include pastoral guidance from the Pope all the way down to the parish pulpit. It might also include organizing mature Catholic couples into a network of consulters, available in each parish to help younger couples discern their path. These volunteer services could be, and should be, promoted by the Pastor, and perhaps be made obligatory in the way that similar arrangements are for Baptismal preparation.

The second area for new foundations is the whole psycho-industrial complex. Ours is a world in which "experts" medicate unhappiness and treat shame as indicator of mental illness. These same "authorities" hold that regular sexual satisfaction is essential to well-being, and that anyone who says they lack a fantasy life is either lying, or sick. These disciplines (psychology, psychiatry, counseling, other "mental health" services) have always been mine fields for seriously Christian people, on both the giving and the receiving end of treatment. The situation is now more perilous than ever, as the properly moral perspective has been driven to the margins of training and practice.

There is nonetheless probably more genuine need for *sound* services of this general type than there ever has been. The stresses of modern living and the dissonance of navigating a secularized world cause people to judge themselves to be unhappy and in need of therapeutic intervention. Frequently, they are.

Chapter 9

The Future of Catholic Higher Education in America

For a full generation the guiding light and the measure of genuine renewal for Catholic colleges and universities in America has been Pope John Paul's Apostolic Constitution on Catholic Universities. Promulgated on the Feast of the Assumption, 1990, *Ex corde ecclesiae* [*"ECE"*] has been the touchstone of *orthodox* criticism of nominally Catholic institutions. *ECE* is also central to the self-understanding of institutions steadfast in their Catholic faith and mission. How *ECE* is doing in America might therefore tell us how much about how American Catholic higher education is doing.

But we face this seeming paradox. Philadelphia's Archbishop Charles Chaput was quoted in *Commonweal* as saying, in a February 2018 talk at Villanova University, that the bishops' implementation of *ECE* in the United States "had no teeth." The American bishops as a whole, on the other hand, say that things are going great.

Which is it?

The most probative piece of evidence is the 2012 United States Conference of Catholic Bishops' review of how well *ECE* had been implemented. The single page which a Google search for the "Final Report for the Ten Year Review of *The Application of Ex Corde Ecclesiae*" turns up is not an Executive Summary. It is the *entire* report. This terse document is based upon a data set limited to conversations between some bishops and university administrators within their dioceses, undertaken between November 2011 and June 2012.

Here are the key findings of the "Report":

[T]he prevailing tone [of these conversations] was positive and the news was good ... The relationship between bishops and presidents on the local level can be characterized as positive and engaged, demonstrating progress on courtesy and cooperation in the last ten years.

[O]ur institutions of Catholic higher education have made definite progress in advancing Catholic identity. Clarity about Catholic identity among college and university leadership has fostered substantive dialogues and cultivated greater mission driven practices across the university. In acknowledging that much progress has been made, we recognize there is still work to be done

... a working group of bishops and presidents will be formed to continue the dialogue about strategic subjects on a national level.

The Report concluded that "the success of the ten-year review provides a clear course for continued dialogue regarding Catholic higher education and its essential contribution to the Church and society."

If *ECE* were a coffee-table book, it could be said to be doing quite well, for it has evidently instigated a lot of edifying conversations. One suspects, however, that the Pope had more in mind than perpetual dialogue when he included in *ECE* several "General Norms" which, the Holy Father wrote, were "to be applied concretely at the local and regional levels by Episcopal Conferences and other Assemblies of Catholic Hierarchy in conformity with the Code of Canon Law and complementary Church legislation."

Still, the American bishops' eminent satisfaction gives one pause, even where so perceptive an observer as Archbishop Chaput has filed a dissenting opinion.

One way of unraveling the seeming paradox would be to hypothesize that enforcement of *ECE* was *meant* to be toothless, because neither the bishops nor the colleges ever *want*ed to actually implement it. So – hypothetically – the bishops are happy to endlessly talk about implementing *ECE*. And Archbishop Chaput is not.

So it is.

I

When the Vatican released for comment in 1985 a draft schema on Catholic universities, the American colleges opposed the whole idea as unnecessary, and even dangerous. (The American responses were collected and published in the bishops' conference's weekly publication, *Origins,* dated April 10, 1986.) The Catholic academic establishment's resistance to episcopal (including papal) involvement goes back further than that, of course, to the Curran affair at Catholic University and the Land o' Lakes ["LoL"] Statement (both 1967), and to the revolt of the theologians (particularly, again, at the Catholic University of America) against *Humane vitae* the next year. Resistance was manifest throughout the 1970s, as the Vatican began developing what would become *Sapientia Christiana,* the Apostolic Constitution on ecclesiastical universities, and the revised Code of Canon Law, which included (in sections 807 – 814 of the text promulgated in 1983) several regulations of universities' Catholic character, including the *mandatum,* which is approximate to an episcopal license for those teaching "theological disciplines."

At least since 1990 the bishops have taken their cues in all academic matters from the colleges. The best that one could say about the bishops is that they might have gone along with a real Application of *ECE* if the colleges would have.

This episcopal docility is most graphically reflected in the bishops' adoption in November 1996 of an *ECE* "Application." This brief document was so bereft of dentures that it makes the current toothless version look fearsome. The Vatican's Congregation for Catholic Education, then headed by Pio Cardinal Laghi, sent it back to the USCCB as – and here one should deftly translate the Vatican diplomatic rhetoric into the vernacular – *unserious* (literally, as no more than a first draft). The bishops had adopted it by a vote of 224 – 6.

The Vatican wanted a "juridical" application. The Americans wanted a "pastoral" approach, in circumstances where "pastoral" was synonymous with "toothless." The heart of this disagreement was the nature of theology, and the practice of it in relation to the truths of the faith and thus to the authority of Scripture and of the Magisterium. This dispute ripened over the *mandatum.* Only at Cardinal Bevilacqua's insistence was any mention of it made in the ill-fated 1996 "Application"; then it was mentioned only in a footnote promising future study of the matter. Most of the academics' sometimes heated, other times rhapsodic, rhetoric about "academic freedom" and "institutional autonomy" has always been another way of saying that they could not stand the *mandatum*.

The Vatican dug in its heels. The American colleges resisted. The bishops were caught in the middle. They were in the in the uncomfortable position of being made by their ecclesiastical superiors to do something which their real masters in the matter – the academics – would not permit them to do. In the event, the bishops genuflected to Rome and caved to the academics.

The enacted "Application" underwent its decennial review in 2012. The "Application," says that "Catholics who teach the theological disciplines are required to have the *mandatum*," with details added to that basic canonical requirement about making the obligation stick. But the preparatory document sent to all the bishops prior to their conversations – also a one-pager – indicates how wobbly it went. Bishops were asked to ask the college presidents: "[H]ow has it been possible to incorporate the norms of The Application ... within the actual situation of the institution?" Included among five categories of asks was "granting the *mandatum*." *Not a word is said of their answers or of the* mandatum *itself in the ten-year report.*

In practice the *mandatum* "requirement" is ignored. In some cases, it is rendered meaningless by granting it on request, or even (I am told) sometimes by bishops giving the *mandatum* to theologians who have not asked for it. It is difficult to say more, because the chanceries will not tell you who has the *mandatum* and who does not. The whole subject is buried; *omerta* is the code.

II

The bishops' enforcement of *ECE* has gone from feckless to farce. There are nonetheless many encouraging signs of faithful renewal in Catholic higher education. A large handful of institutions, such as Franciscan University, Ave Maria, Benedictine, and the University of Mary (among others), have taken to heart the task of providing a genuine Catholic education while also offering majors that prepare young men and women to take their places as Catholic laity in the workforce and as citizens. These institutions are treasures. May they be fruitful and multiply.

The sobering fact, however, is that the *total* enrollment in *all* the colleges recommended by the Cardinal Newman Society (to take just one index of committed Catholic orthodoxy) is several thousand fewer than the enrollment just at Saint Leo's in Florida, or at DePaul in Chicago, neither of which is likely to crack the Newman list any time soon.

Another welcome development since the turn of the millennium has been the establishment of so many Catholic institutes, study centers, and think tanks on or near secular campuses. These foundations, of which the University of Chicago's Lumen Christi Institute is a prototype, have brought Catholic education to where so many Catholics are actually going to college – non-Catholic institutions. These foundations, along with the intellectually (as well as spiritually) ambitious Newman Centers on secular campuses (at the Universities of Illinois, Kansas, and Virginia, for example), provide a substantial measure of the Catholic education available at steadfast colleges like Steubenville or Benedictine, and more than is available on some nominally Catholic campuses.

The more sobering fact is that the market for genuinely Catholic higher education is now quite limited. There are many reasons why this is so. Secularization of society and the comparative affordability of public colleges are two reasons. Another is the ambient reduction of collegiate education to a combination of *pabulum* and vocational preparation, a development so widespread and so intractable that it has taken many Catholic colleges and universities in its maws. This devolution of higher "education" into pap-and-bread shows no sign of letting them go. These considerable obstacles to faithful renewal might be overcome, though, were it not for the surrounding cultural collapse which this entire book seeks to describe and to analyze: in a social world which so prizes solipsistic self-expression it is very difficult indeed to interest young people in an education which not only focuses their minds and hearts on divine realities, but on preparation for a life of discipleship. And long gone is the spur that credible episcopal authority on Catholic higher education might have provided.

To say that the market for Catholic higher education (or for anything else) is limited is to say that not many people find it appealing enough to purchase. The situation is worse than that, for genuine Catholic higher education is nearly unintelligible to the teens who shop for colleges by considering curb appeal, sports teams' buzz, amenities worthy of cruise ships, and post-graduation job prospects. This "consumerist" approach to higher education, and the catering to it by so many colleges, constitutes a market in which the appeal of *any* genuine learning – much more the Catholic kind of it – is marginal. There is no way to sugar-coat it: real Catholic education lacks a certain "wow" factor.

No wonder that enrollment consultants invariably tell faithful colleges with flagging enrollments to lighten up. Downplay the whole Catholic thing. Be less religious and more "spiritual." Make sure you have co-ed dorms, a rock-climbing wall, and that the professors prepare digests of all the readings they assign.

Seriously Catholic parents do not think that, if Jack wants no part of a real Catholic education, he should be made to get one anyway (or at least have to foot the bill for State U. himself). These parents might send their children to Notre Dame. But most parents who do so do so mostly for the reasons that their neighbors send their kids to Duke: to study at a US News & World Report elite school amongst their peers from Charles Murray's "Belmont," all of whom want the valuable credential and network connections that come from doing so.

The appetite for a real Catholic education is an *acquired* one. It is developed by the cultivation of a tutored desire for it. It is as if one has to *be properly educated in order to want to be properly educated,* which is probably true of liberal education generally, too. Demand for either must be stimulated, or contrived, and presented to people as a kind of moral imperative: it is just what good people do. Catholic higher education may not be eye-catching in the showroom; it lacks a certain "wow" factor. Buy it anyway and later one will agree that it was not a luxury option, but something like a necessity. A genuine Catholic education is the pearl of great price. It just so happens to be one that few today want to purchase. Properly educated parents might, too. But today's Catholic parents of college-aged teens are themselves the products (or victims) of a radically defective higher education, at least when it comes to cultivating a sense of discipleship.

It might be worth recalling here that the robust enrollments at Catholic colleges in yesteryear (often at fifty percent, and occasionally higher, of the total number of Catholics attending college or university), resulted partly from a peculiarly potent stimulus, namely, muscular episcopal salesmanship. One important reason why the colleges were then full of Catholics is that bishops preached about the crucial importance of patronizing the Church's institutions. Some bishops even enforced, during the first half of the twentieth century, a disciplinary requirement that Catholics obtain pastoral permission to attend a non-Catholic institution. Bishops worried about the religious indifferentism at public schools and about outright hostility to Catholics at some private institutions. They worried, too, about mundane temptations outside Catholic auspices. Throughout those decades there was even a lively controversy among bishops over whether Newman Centers should be encouraged, lest they make going to a non-Catholic college appealing and spiritually plausible.

III

The heart of the episcopal sales pitch then was this message: Catholic higher education fits one out for the challenges of being an adult layman or laywoman in the mid-twentieth century. That should be the pitch today, save that we are talking about the twenty-first century now. But that does *not* imply that today's Catholic colleges should try to mimic their ancestor institutions. Not at all. One reason is that the prevailing understanding of the lay life was then quite different than it is now; the Vatican Council happened since the Catholic colleges were full in the last century and the laity's task in building the Kingdom transformed by it. (We shall return to this topic later in this Chapter, and in Chapter Ten.) Besides, ecclesiastical discipline is not an appropriate guide to college choice. Catholic teens and their parents should choose colleges for themselves. But do they know what they should be looking for? Have pastors catechized them about the moral responsibilities incumbent upon the overwhelming majority of young Catholics as they enter adulthood, namely, the obligations to acquire an adult faith, to prepare for the lay apostolate, and to discern one's personal vocation? Have parents and teens been instructed about how the whole collegiate experience can aid, or hinder, each one's discharge of those serious moral duties? Are they prepared, in other words, to conscientiously select a college?

IV

Almost certainly not. Instead the party line adopted by the episcopacy, in union with the Catholic academic establishment, flattens the demand curve for real Catholic higher education. Its depressing effects fall into two categories. For those parents and high-schoolers who are interested in Catholic higher education, the party line dilutes attempts – by the Cardinal Newman Society, by the *National Catholic Register*, and by anybody else – to steer them to places that will deliver the real deal. We should not judge these parents and kids too harshly for believing what a phalanx of professors, presidents, and prelates all profess to be true: things are fine at all the Catholic colleges and universities. If you doubt it, read (and it will take but a moment) the bishops' ten-year review of how well *ECE* is doing on campus: it is all going great. Just pick a Catholic college that strikes your fancy. And we should not be surprised to discover that a generation of Catholics who have been poorly catechized and never educated by their pastors about what a Catholics collegiate education is supposed to be, and what it is for, think of a Catholic higher education as what you could, and would, get at any college, with convenient Mass times thrown in.

Yes, some pastors today still dare to speak the truth. But not many, and few of them are as fearless as Charles Chaput. Many of the silent bishops know the truth about the dismal state of Catholic higher education today; it is plain enough to see. These men will not parrot the party-line. But they cannot change the course of the national conference, and they are reluctant to speak *so* forthrightly about the dismal state of things as to implicitly rebuke their brother bishops, and the academic establishment, for slack judgment, roseate optimism, and for straight-out duplicity. These alert pastors remain on the sidelines, muffled if not mute.

Here is the party line's second sort of effect: good pastors do not tutor the faithful about the true nature and great value of a genuine Catholic higher education – and how it can promote living up to what morality and the faith require of each one of us.

The party-line is a pastoral catastrophe. It makes no difference at all that bishops and college presidents occasionally have pleasant chats. Bishops seem to think that, because they may have no direct role in governing the local Catholic college (which typically is civilly incorporated with a lay board of trustees in charge), they can do no more than occasionally "dialogue" with presidents about Catholic "identity." Over the years many bishops have gladly reported that, because they maintained such a "good relationship" with a Catholic college, they were able to talk a President out of some scandalous scheme, such as awarding an honorary degree to a pro-choice politician. These bishops are unwittingly boasting about being patsies in a protection racket: colleges refrain from breaking the Church's windows in return for episcopal payouts, where the bishop ignores a host of other scandalous acts. In truth, bishops have an essential role to play in authoritatively *judging* whether *any* institution or association in the Official Catholic Directory belongs there. In other words, the bishop is solely in charge of authoritatively judging whether a college in his diocese is truly Catholic.

This grave duty is made most explicit, and certainly obligatory, by Canon 808: "Even if it is in fact Catholic no university is to bear the title or name of Catholic university without the consent of competent ecclesiastical authority." This is not the charge of a consultant. Nor is it that of an avuncular senior advisor. It is the role of a spiritual governor. There is no doubt whatsoever, too, that civil law courts in this country would enforce a bishop's decision to delete an institution from the Catholic Directory, and his decree that thereafter it never identify itself as "Catholic." Bishops must fulfill this limited but indispensable role in governing the college as part and parcel of his obligation to govern his whole diocese.

They must go over the colleges' heads and speak directly to the people. Pastors must jumpstart demand for a genuine Catholic higher education by teaching all those in their spiritual care what college is for and what a Catholic college should be doing. Bishops must also go over the colleges' heads to the American Catholic donor class. For the second main reason why Catholic colleges decades ago were filled with the faithful is that the price tag was right, even for working-class families. Now, not so much.

The reasons why a Catholic higher education used to be so affordable – crushing teaching loads for barely paid religious faculty and underpaid lay professors, as well as very modest accommodations and amenities – are no longer available. Because the vast majority of Catholic colleges and universities are now tuition-driven, they are always teetering between red and black at the end of the fiscal year. Philanthropy is the solution.

America's Catholics need to make Catholic higher education affordable – again. Fortunately, they can. The American Catholic community is unquestionably capable of making a real Catholic collegiate education affordable for all those who want one. (Notre Dame's thirteen billion-dollar endowment – and growing – alone proves the point.) Re-directing the contributions of vain baby-boomer donors from underwriting an unnecessary "event space" or a boutique gym at a rich university to supporting fellowships at a struggling college will be hard pastoral work. It is certainly true that some or even many gifts currently being made to higher ed should be directed elsewhere, to meet more pressing material and even spiritual needs of the flock. Nevertheless those who are called to give to higher education ought to be giving *much* more judiciously than they are.

The sooner America's bishops begin catechizing the rich about their stewardship obligations, the better. The anticipated result would resemble the Church's commitment today to making elementary and secondary education widely available, and affordable. And this redevelopment project must include ample resources for the off-campus institutes and Newman Centers at non-Catholic institutions. For many of America's Catholic will, and should, conscientiously select them: the programs of study there, comparative affordability, and proximity to home might all (or each) make the choice the right one for many Catholic teens. Consider, for example, that there is no Catholic college or university in several states, including Arizona and South Carolina.

Launching such an ambitious project calls for a compelling description of Catholic higher education and the moral necessity of patronizing and underwriting it. *ECE* does not supply it.

V

So far we have barely scratched the surface of the question: what is the state of Catholic higher education in America in 2018? After all, Catholic higher education is much more than those 220 or so colleges and universities listed in the Official Catholic ("Kenedy") Directory. Only a tiny fraction of the Catholics in post-secondary schools are enrolled in them. Somewhere between 90 and 95 percent are enrolled elsewhere, in public and non-Catholic private institutions. Add in that only half of those enrolled in Catholic colleges and universities "self-identify" as Catholic (a percentage in sharp decline over the last few decades, and almost certain to shrink further), and it is even more clear that any consideration of how Catholic higher education is doing – and where it should go – must venture well beyond the official Kenedy Directory.

And beyond *ECE*. There Pope John Paul II was almost exclusively concerned with Catholic institutions and so with a tiny percentage of Catholics seeking higher education. *ECE* does not say much about the great majority of Catholic institutions, either. It is principally about the *modern Catholic research university*. But those institutions in particular are not listening to the Holy Father. With the partial exception of the bishops' own university, Catholic University of America, is there a research university that is living up to its Catholic mission? No other is listed in the Newman Guide. *ECE* is principally about the dynamic, creative intellectual life of the university faculty, considered individually and as a community of scholars. It is also about the constructive if not vital role that community, and the university as a whole, should play in its host society and culture.

In *ECE* the Pope described the Catholic university as "a community of scholars representing various branches of human knowledge and an academic institution where Catholicism is vitally present and operative," here citing the International Federation of Catholic Universities' 1972 document "The Catholic University in the Modern World." (IFCU was a partnership between the Vatican department of education and Catholic colleges throughout the world.) The Pope wrote in *ECE* that the mission of the university is the "continuous quest for truth through its research, and the preservation and communication of knowledge for the good of society. A Catholic university participates in this mission with its own specific characteristics and purposes."

ECE identified four characteristics which every Catholic university must possess; all of these Pope John Paul II took *verbatim* form the 1972 IFCU document. So, the American bishops' 1993 starting point in thinking about implementing *ECE,* as they found it in *ECE* : "According to *Ex corde ecclesiae,* 'the objective of a Catholic university is to assure in an institutional manner a Christian presence in a university world confronting the great problems of society and culture.'"

These passages and the many like them in *ECE* locate it firmly within a stream of reflections instigated by Vatican II. It is the document fore-shadowed in the Council's treatment of education, *Gravissimum educationis* [*GE*], but not delivered until 1990. *GE* was almost entirely about elementary and secondary education, about pupils, schools, and parents. Only a few paragraphs of it address higher education. These brief passages in *GE* are best summarized in these excerpts: "The Church is concerned also with … colleges and universities. In those schools dependent on her she intends that by their very constitution individual subjects be pursued according to their own principles, method, and liberty of scientific inquiry, in such a way that an ever deeper understanding in these fields may be obtained and that, as questions that are new and current are raised and investigations carefully made according to the example of the doctors of the Church and especially of St. Thomas Aquinas, there may be a deeper realization of the harmony of faith and science. Thus there is accomplished a public, enduring and pervasive influence of the Christian mind in the furtherance of culture."

Here in *GE* is *ECE in utero*. In *ECE* Pope John Paul II wrote that "the mission of the university is the continuous quest for truth through its research, and the preservation and communication of knowledge for the good of society. A Catholic university participates in this mission with its own specific characteristics and purposes." "Since the objective of a Catholic University is to assure in an institutional manner a Christian presence in the university world confronting the great problems of society and culture."

VI

ECE is best understood, not as anything like a blueprint for Catholic higher education, but as an attempt to implement *Gaudium et spes* [*GS*], the "Constitution on the Church in the Modern World," by and through the activities of the Catholic university. It is no small irony that the document lately taken to be the alter ego of *ECE* – the Theodore Hesburgh-orchestrated *LoL* Statement – is squarely within the same stream of reflections. No doubt *its* authors *thought* of their work as applying *GS* to their own institutions. Commemorating in 2017 the fiftieth anniversary of that statement, Notre Dame President Fr. John Jenkins wrote in *America* magazine that *ECE* "can be viewed as the result of the dialog begun by the Lakes statement, echoing some of its themes, while providing a corrective to others."

How could this be? In the United States these two visions of the contemporary Catholic university – *LoL* and *ECE* – have been sharply opposed, as two battle flags under which antagonistic visions of Catholic higher education have warred for hearts and minds. Fr. Jenkins is right. *ECE* and *LoL* have much more in common than not. Each is mainly concerned with the social role of the Catholic scholar and of Catholic research institutions, as an intellectual force among others, and as a catalyst for social change. *ECE* and *LoL* could both be neatly folded into the 1972 treatment of "The Catholic University in the Modern World," with only the limited but important canonical commitments of *ECE* appended.

Contributing to the American Church's embrace of *LoL* was the widespread conviction that direct episcopal involvement in academic matters was not fruitful. Such interventions were indeed episodic and very often ham-handed. There is ample reason to criticize a pastoral practice which too frequently consisted of brief phone calls during which His Excellency – often with little more than a gut feeling or second-hand information – peremptorily informed a university president that this or that speaker was not to be permitted on campus, or even that a professor be fired. Especially as the percentage of lay faculty at Catholic institutions expanded in the 1960s, a thorough reconsideration of the role of episcopal authority on campuses *was* needed. *LoL*'s rejection of all such "external" interference was, however, just as peremptory and unfruitful. Fr. Hesburgh and his mostly Jesuit confreres at Land o'Lakes (though including Theodore McCarrick, then President of the Catholic University of Puerto Rico) took a blunderbuss to a task which required a scalpel.

More efficiently fueling the ambient unease with episcopal involvement, though, was the sort of intellectual inferiority complex voiced by the leading historian of American Catholic higher education, Monsignor John Tracy Ellis. In 1966, the American Council on Education issued a study that failed to uncover a single Catholic university with a "distinguished" or even "strong" graduate department among the three-hundred-plus Catholic universities and colleges in the United States. This prompted Monsignor Ellis, according to the 2019 recollection of veteran Catholic editor and journalist Kenneth Woodward, to say to him (Woodward): "I don't think we should have more than three Catholic universities in this country, "one on the Atlantic seaboard, one in the Middle West and one on the West Coast."

Note the focal point of Ellis's observation *universities* and, within them, *graduate education* as the *secular academy* would have them. Not even Ellis could have imagined that all of the American Catholics who wanted a Catholic higher education could be squeezed onto those three campuses. Nor did he give an apparent thought to the hundreds of smaller Catholic colleges, where the vast majority of America's Catholics would receive their collegiate education. Simply put: wholesale reform of Catholic higher *education* in America was to a significant extent rooted in worries about graduate studies in Catholic research institutions, compared to secular peer schools. It surely seems too that much of the conversation about the matter since the 1960s has similarly been about the upper echelons of *university* life and not about collegiate education at all.

VII

It is telling that in the walk-up to the "Application" of *ECE* to the United States, there was agreement across the aisle between colleges and prelates that *ECE* was a terrific document – until the Pope got to the part about juridical implementation, and there mainly Canon 812. To those riding on this train of thought, the *mandatum* would naturally become – as it did for the academic establishment as well as the bishops – the tail wagging the dog. In the great work of conversing with the wider intellectual world and of trying to save the rest of it, the ecclesiastical credentialing of theologians – if indeed "theology" should continue to be thought of in connection with the Church at all – would be a footnote, if not an impediment to achieving those large aims.

It is no mystery therefore why the Americans not only opposed the *mandatum* all along, but also considered it entirely negotiable, even after Rome insisted on it. It is also a bit mysterious why anyone, including the Pope, would make the *mandatum* requirement somehow *indispensable* to the Catholic university doing the grand extramural work set before it in *ECE*. After all, theology is not a required course at many Catholic colleges, and ECE does not plainly require that all students be instructed in it. It says only that "Courses in Catholic doctrine are to be *made available* to all students" (my emphasis).

Now it rather seems that ECE's rich vision of the Catholic research university and its place in society is *practically* incompatible with providing a true Catholic education to its undergraduates. The sources of incompatibility are many. The commitment of faculty members to their own scholarly work and reputations indenture them to a secular guild with little or no sympathy for things Catholic. Commitments to graduate students drain time from care for undergraduates. Departments competing for the best prospective graduate students – themselves aspiring apprentices in the guild – must double-down on their secular prestige. Prospective faculty hires, ideally (these days) from secular schools such as Harvard or Yale, are not going to warm to a Catholic university that takes chastity, for example, as it should.

Now, there is nothing *necessarily* incompatible about being both a profoundly serious Catholic intellectual and being a fully engaged, respected participant in the wide scholarly conversation about, say, worthwhile literature or the origins of the universe or government family policy or the history of religion in America or same-sex "marriage." But anyone who has lately tried to unite these aspirations will tell you that it is a steep uphill climb, with trade-offs all along the way, and then at the end the discovery that one's lamp is hidden under a bushel. The sad fact is that in the last generation or so the cause of higher education for America's Catholic has been doubly ill-served: too much talk about what makes a Catholic research university, a project which has proved to be empirically unavailable, alongside too little talk about how to do what is possible, namely, offer a genuine Catholic education at the colleges willing to tackle that task.

The understanding of a Catholic university throughout these documents (*ECE, LoL*, the IFCU paper, the bishops' iterations of an "Application") is heavily mortgaged to the prevailing wider understanding of the modern research university. They all understand the Catholic university as a particular inflection of the modern research university which makes such an institution *Catholic, as species within the* genus. The Catholic university is enjoined to stay in tune with, and to be a fully respected member of, the contemporary academic scene. It is also enjoined to help solve the political and cultural problems of its host society. This latter injunction would immerse the Catholic university in myriad shifting contingencies and a now-bitter partisan rancor. Whatever might have been the wisdom thirty or forty (or fifty) years ago of a clarion call to heed these two external forces, now it is plainly an injunction to immerse the university's Catholic character in acids of radical secularism and even of irrationality. Today, a nearly militant independence of purpose, if not of mind, has to be an essential feature of a genuinely Catholic college or university.

VIII

Vatican II *should* have transformed Catholic higher education. And it did. The Council's legacy as a matter of fact was compromise, dissent, and secularization. The Council *should* have occasioned documents about colleges with a palpable sense of hopeful renewal. In the event we got *Land o' Lakes*, and all of its often-vapid talk about the next great Catholic research institution, one that its secular peers would respect. The Council Fathers' work *should* have been consummated by a papal intervention which deepened and concretized the new foundations for Catholic higher education which they articulated. Instead we got an inadequate, and too-long delayed, papal response in *ECE*.

The basic goal of a distinctly Catholic collegiate education is indicated in *GE*: "[A] public, enduring and pervasive influence of the Christian mind in the furtherance of culture and the *students of these institutions are molded into men truly outstanding in their training, ready to undertake weighty responsibilities in society and witness to the faith in the world*" (emphasis added). Yes, preparation for the lay apostolate is the central aim of a distinctly Catholic higher education. How should that broad aspiration be concretized? In *ECE* the Holy Father spoke of the presence of so many laity in the university as a *"sign of hope and as a confirmation of the irreplaceable lay vocation in the Church and in the world."* But what are the distinctive elements *of* education for the lay apostolate?

These distinctive elements have to *go beyond* (that is: include but surpass or transcend) technical mastery of a discipline-*cum*-personal piety; otherwise, there would be a Catholic education wherever a good chapel is located near a non-Catholic campus. Life can be good for a serious Catholic student at a public university which teaches engineering well and has an excellent parish next door. But a good spiritual life plus a good engineering degree does not equal a Catholic education. Much less does a degree from a nominally Catholic college.

The distinctively Catholic elements of a higher education cannot be entirely supplied by a curricular module or summer seminar, as if the Catholic components were affixed to what would otherwise be the schooling on offer at State U. These distinctives are well promoted by discrete projects, such as courses, seminars, lectures, service opportunities, extra-curricular activities: all so many "Catholic" moments in the course of an undergraduate's collegiate career. The distinctively Catholic elements are not reducible, however, to such moments. They surpass all particulars and must suffuse the entire enterprise.

It is important to note that an energetic Newman Center or nearby institute such as Lumen Christi can supply much of the distinctive education, if students are willing to commit to more than attending the occasional lecture. Offering the occasional lecture or discussion session is useful in itself. But it is better as an introduction – and invitation – to take up the serious business of educating oneself for the lay apostolate. Catholic moments, on or off campus, will not themselves do.

It would not be wrong to say that inculcating a "Catholic worldview" is that distinctive purpose. But that project is vague and incomplete. Inculcating a "Catholic worldview" is in any event *included* within the interlocking and reinforcing purposes of a distinctly Catholic higher education. That distinctive purpose is not coming to know the "Catholic intellectual tradition," much less is it a deep dive into particular parts of that tradition, such as Thomism or early Church history. Studying the "Catholic intellectual tradition" consists mainly in studying writers: the Fathers, or Bonaventure, or de Lubac. Scholars make careers out of studying Lonergan or John Courtney Murray. Some of those scholars are not Catholic and may not be believers at all. Requiring students to study, say, Aquinas or von Balthasar is in itself fine. But to do so without very critically evaluating whether, for example, von Balthasar is *right* about heaven, or Aquinas *right* about the death penalty, is not enough.

It is most perspicuous to identify the core of a distinctively Catholic education as the *faith,* or as *the truths of the faith.* Pope John Paul wrote in *ECE* that the Catholic university's "privileged task" is to "unite existentially by intellectual effort two orders of reality" often thought to be opposed, namely, "the search for truth and the certainty of already knowing the fount of truth." What the Holy Father had precisely in mind is unclear. But whatever it exactly is, it is subsumed within, or incidentally accomplished, by dedication to that core. The truths of the faith include those accessible to unaided reason, some of which are confirmed (explicitly or implicitly) by revelation, as well as truths accessible only by faith, through a faith that is itself *reasonable* to hold, and which truths can only be understood and developed by use of our reason.

The Second Vatican Council founded the renewal of Catholic higher education upon a triple refraction of this core. That tripod supporting (or specifying) its core in truth was: the extraordinary development in the Church's understanding of adult Catholic faith in *Dignitatis humanae,* as a free decision to adhere to the truth, a whole turning of the person that is uniquely and deeply personal; the breathtaking teaching on the lay apostolate in *Apostolicam actuositatem [AA]*; and the rediscovery of the concept of *personal vocation*, which had lain buried for centuries under the sediment of clericalism.

The first leg of the tripod so deepened and universalized the gospel truth about *metanoia* that it was tantamount to a development of doctrine. The second was a doctrinal innovation. The third revived a theological corpse. Each was, therefore and in its own way, startlingly *new*. Together they constituted a transformative impetus for Catholic higher education, for they converge upon that span of life when the teen leaves (if not literally, then practically) home and prepares to take up the responsibilities of an adult member of the lay faithful. *Every* Catholic, college-bound or not, is obliged to make this transition. *Every* Catholic person needs substantial assistance making it, especially because of the intellectual shoals which a complex secularized culture puts in the way to mature faith – and most especially where the young Catholic is going to college. *Then* it is essential that he or she be accompanied on that journey by a faith-filled Catholic higher education.

Let me say a little more about each leg of the tripod of renewal. Because we shall consider carefully the last two components in the next chapter, here we shall say just a bit about how these crucial spiritual realities pertain most directly to a collegiate education.

IX

The Council's Declaration on Religious Freedom (*DH*, as the reader will recall form chapters two and three) is justly acclaimed for its development of doctrine on the right of non-Catholics to the public manifestation of their religions, even in a polity predominantly populated by Catholics. This welcome change is probably the only (strictly speaking) development of doctrine in the document. But *DH* is powered throughout by its fresh, keen recognition that (as the Council Fathers phrased it) "[t]he truth cannot impose itself except by virtue of its own truth, as it makes its entrance into the mind at once quietly and with power." The Fathers added that it is "in accordance with their dignity as persons – that is, beings endowed with reason and free will and therefore privileged to bear personal responsibility – that all men should be at once impelled by nature and also bound by a moral obligation to seek the truth, especially religious truth. They are also bound to adhere to the truth, once it is known, and to order their whole lives in accord with the demands of truth." This pairing of existential freedom with abiding moral duty is the challenge of coming to a faith-of-one's-own, both *mine* and *true,* indeed, *mine-because-true.*

This is *adult* faith. It is *adult* not only because it is one's own (for even children have a genuinely personal faith), but because it is acquired and held by dint of personal conviction of its truth, and not because of habit, conformity to family ways, social advantage, or parental authority. It is also a more critical and sophisticated and integral grasp of the faith than is possible during childhood. It is an adult *faith* in two senses: that of holding certain propositions as true by dint of faith, as well as enjoyment of that intimate relationship with the Master, which we call "faith."

The journey to adult faith is surely personal, individual, and interior. An education fitted to the challenge is nonetheless essential, in or out of a collegiate setting. A college or university education in America today is certain to throw up numerous obstacles, including the student's first serious encounters with a slew of deformations, including cultural relativism, evolution, a suitably critical approach to reading Scripture, the problem of evil, and the apparent – or at least reported – sufficiency of a personal "spirituality" as an alternative to religion.

In the "Decree on the Apostolate of the Laity" [*AA*] the Council

Fathers provided a theological account faithful to revelation but fresh in its departure from centuries of clericalism, which made sense of what had been practically developing within the Church for several decades, namely, the increased role of the laity in social and political affairs consciously as *Catholics.* But even in its most celebrated moments, such as Pius XI's christening of Catholic Action in the 1920s, activist laity invariably were described as *participating in the apostolate of the hierarchy,* and so operating in the temporal sphere at the direction of their pastors. These words from *AA* in 1965 were unprecedented, and challenging: "The laity are called by God to exercise their apostolate in the world like leaven with the ardor of the spirit of Christ." In this they "share in the priestly, prophetic, and royal office" of the Master. These shares are not derived from participation in the apostolate of the hierarchy. Rather, the laity "have their own share in the mission of the whole people of God in the Church and in the world." This is their "right and duty," rooted in their union with Christ the head.

This task is a form of faith-filled service. Performing it is possible only with the grace of the sacraments. A fervent prayer life is essential. But one more thing (at least) is needed: understanding, or knowledge. To be sure, a Catholic need not receive the sort of advanced higher education that a bachelor's degree offers in order to acquire this knowledge and thus this adult faith; were that true, most of the Church's saints would not pass muster, notwithstanding that some (the Little Flower among them) championed their faith as a childlike faith. But the understanding or knowledge typically constitutive of the *adult* faith of which I am speaking nevertheless has to be born out of critical reflection on the *reasonableness* of faith and, to some extent, has to be able to give a reason for one's faith *in response to objections*, as St. Peter reminded his flock (1 Pet 3:15).

In *this* sense, what is needed to perform this form of faith-filled service is precisely what a genuinely Catholic education can well or even paradigmatically provide: a full-orbed Catholic worldview, wherein the connections and pathways between the Catholic faith and the various autonomous spheres of modern life (science, self, sex, economy, politics, and use of force) are illumined. Indeed, the single concept of being "leaven" within the temporal order reveals that each member of the laity is to integrate the gospel with all his undertakings: scholarly, professional, social, political, economic, family. Doing so requires learning, to be sure. But it depends too upon models of such integration. For college students, these models would have to include their professors, not only in theology, but also and more importantly, in the disciplines related to temporal affairs – business, nursing, psychology, science, teaching, and various pre-professional studies.

Finally, Vatican II rediscovered and revivified the idea of *personal vocation*. It is what Cardinal Newman talked about beautifully in words quoted by Pope Benedict in 2010 during Newman's beatification ceremonies: "God has created *me* to do him some definite service. He has committed some work to *me* which he has not committed to another. I have my mission." "My mission" is a distinct and unrepeatable assignment. One must *discern* this unique calling, this individualized way of collaborating with Jesus. This discernment includes prayerfully identifying one's gifts, one's opportunities, one's training, and, most importantly, the needs of others within the circle within reach, so that one may act in a helpful way.

These three distinctive purposes of Catholic higher education – the Vatican II tripod – are so tightly related that the meaning of each to some extent bleeds into the others. For example: an adult faith includes seeing to it about personal vocation and how to live as lay man or woman in the real world. Who could discern one's personal vocation without an adult faith? Who could spend a lifetime endeavoring to be leaven in an increasingly godless wider world without the resources provided by an adult faith, and the serenity which is a by-product of conscientious discernment? The synergy is powerful, as each of the three purposes depends upon deepening sense of all three.

X

What might an operational core Catholic higher education actually look like? How might the *truths of the faith* be made foundational to a program which promoted the undergraduate's transition to adult faith, preparation for the lay apostolate, and discernment of his or her personal vocation?

My answer is to make select documents of Vatican II a required core curriculum. To it Catholic colleges could add additional core requirements, up to the limit case where almost the whole four-year program would be a required liberal arts curriculum. Other Catholic colleges could add a modest additional core, and then make ample opportunity for practical majors (nursing, business, physical therapy, teaching, or architecture), as well as majors in the humanities, social, and natural sciences. There is nothing like a one-size-fits-all to Catholic higher education *in the round*. But something like what is sketched below is an invariable core of any genuine Catholic higher education. Catholic institutes and Newman Centers should, in addition to their other activities, try to deliver as much as possible of it, too.

The core I recommend would consist of eight three-credit courses, one each semester over four years. The entire reading list for each of the first six semesters would be one or two of the Council documents, with very limited additional assignments as needed for explanation and illustration – and *not* for interpretation or "dialogue." The point is to let the faith be heard, by letting the Council speak. Critical discussion of these documents is of course the objective. The many legitimate questions about translation from the original Latin, historical derivation of leading themes and propositions, as well as how best to give coherent content to vague parts and *lacunae* in them, should be taken up by the teacher and discussion of them led by him or her. A seminar-sized group of students with ample opportunity for discussion and debate is, too, essential.

The precise order in which the documents should be taken up is debatable. It would seem best to begin, however, with *Dei verbum*, the "Dogmatic Constitution on Divine Revelation," so that students can learn immediately that there is *truth* in and about religion, that God has chosen to reveal Himself to humankind in a way that has been reliably transmitted from the apostles to us, and that the Church safeguards and expounds that truth. These realities are foundational to further study. The sooner that the students learn how to read Scripture in a properly critical way, the better.

The second and third semesters would best be devoted to exploring, in one, the nature of the Church and thus *Lumen gentium* ("The Constitution on the Church"), and in the other, *DH* along with *Nostra aetate*, the "Declaration on the Relation of the Church with Non-Christian Religions." The priority of *Lumen Gentium* is probably self-evident. The importance of the other two documents lies mostly here in their invitation to students to engage, sooner rather than later, the relationships among natural religion, positive or revealed religion, human freedom, and respect for the conscientious but mistaken religious beliefs of other people. The fourth semester almost certainly then should be devoted to *Sacrosanctum Concilium*, the "Constitution on the Sacred Liturgy." The Mass is the source and summit of the Christian life. Enough said.

Junior year would be the time to take up, first, *GS* and then *AA*. The first situates the student within the Church as it conceptualizes its relationship to the "modern world." The latter of course brings that engagement home to the individual student, as he or she begins to concretely consider now, after nearly three years of college, how to be "leaven" in the temporal order. The seventh semester should be devoted to a suitably critical study of the leading magisterial documents of what is conventionally called "Catholic Social Thought."

The final semester is the time to challenge students to develop their own resolve about how, and how faithfully, they shall witness to the faith after they go forth. Students on the eve of commencement might best be required to consider lastly two sections (38 – 39) of *GS* that pastors and theologians have almost entirely ignored since the Council:

> Therefore, while we are warned that it profits a man nothing if he gain the whole world and lose himself, the expectation of a new earth must not weaken but rather stimulate our concern for cultivating this one. For here grows the body of a new human family, a body which even now is able to give some kind of foreshadowing of the new age. Hence, while earthly progress must be carefully distinguished from the growth of Christ's kingdom, to the extent that the former can contribute to the better ordering of human society, it is of vital concern to the Kingdom of God.
>
> For after we have obeyed the Lord, and in His Spirit nurtured on earth the values of human dignity, brotherhood and freedom, and indeed all the good fruits of our nature and enterprise, we will find them again, but freed of stain, burnished and transfigured, when Christ hands over to the Father: "a kingdom eternal and universal, a kingdom of truth and life, of holiness and grace, of justice, love and peace." On this earth that Kingdom is already present in mystery. When the Lord returns it will be brought into full flower.

Ideally, a Catholic college would require *all* faculty to rotate in and out of teaching these classes, on the view that if these are the things that every student at a Catholic college should be immersed in, so too every faculty member. A transitional arrangement might be to have the best and most-qualified teachers teach these seminars, with other professors encouraged to sit in, and to have perhaps weekly evening receptions where students and faculty are very strongly encouraged to come and discuss the week's readings. Doing so would establish a community of learning and of mutual aid in exploring life's challenges, one big campus conversation about living the faith in contemporary society.

It is probably easy to see by now that *ECE*'s stated norm that Catholics constitute at least a bare majority of faculty at a Catholic college is considerably short of the mark. No doubt a faith-filled theology faculty is essential to the educational project at hand as well. The *mandatum* would be a sign of its presence. But it is easy to see too that having faithful Catholic throughout the faculty, in all of the disciplines, is possibly even more important to preparing Catholics to be Gospel leaven in the temporal order.

Conclusion

Renewal of Catholic higher education is not a just noble ideal or a desirable aspiration. It is an important obligation. At its core is the perennial faith. Animating its instantiation in institutions – Catholic colleges and universities; Catholic institutes and Newman Centers – are the moral duties of everyone. These duties include those of the young to fit themselves for the life of active adult lay men and women. They include the obligations of everyone else, from bishops to donors to parents to educators on down, to make readily available a real Catholic education to all who want one.

Chapter 10

Personal Vocation and the Laity's Call to Redeem the Temporal Order

When one hears the term "vocation" in everyday conversation, it is usually a reference to someone's job. A "vocational" high school is one in which students learn a trade or occupation. When someone speaks about the "vocational" trend among the nation's universities, the speaker means that these institutions are forsaking a genuine collegiate education for the sake of making students ready for the job market. Occasionally one hears a secular profession – medicine, law, and the like – called a "vocation" (or, synonymously, a "calling"). We often describe what we do when we are *not* working as an *"a*vocation" – golfing, quilting, playing Mario Kart, and the like.

"Vocation" has always had an additional, distinctive meaning for Catholics. In addition to these ambient usages, Catholics distinctively have spoken about a "vocation" as something which priests and sisters have but which the vast majority of Catholics lack, namely: a "calling" from the Lord to serve Him. The "vocations" crisis has to do with having too few priests. When we pray for "vocations" at Mass we pray that more young men and women will respond to God's call of them to religious life.

This way of thinking and speaking was captured vividly in the words of Monsignor George Talbot, the English hierarchy's man in Rome back when the laity supported John Henry Newman against the English episcopacy. The noted Catholic author and journalist Russell Shaw related a question to which the Monsignor supplied his own answer: "What is the province of the laity? To hunt, to shoot, to entertain. These matters they understand. But to meddle with ecclesiastical matters they have no right at all."[1]

By the late twentieth-century this understanding of "vocations" had mightily contributed to a culture of *clericalism* within the Church; hence the subtitle of Shaw's fine book: *Clericalism and the Catholic Laity.* At the dawn of the twenty-first century, we discovered that this culture of clericalism contributed in some significant measure to the crisis of sexual misconduct among priests. (How much it caused the crisis I leave to others to ascertain.) The broader understanding of Catholicism in which this clericalism flourished included, perhaps principally, the thought that the holiness which is the main thing in life has to do with overtly religious things, such as the sacraments and what goes on in and around churches. Priests are in charge of all these things; therefore, they are very holy. Sanctity is for them and for nuns, because they spend their days in prayer and in other patently religious undertakings.

The layman's lot was, evidently, to make the trains run on time, to perfect his bow-hunting skills, and to devise ever-more enchanting entertainments. The idea that *everyone* could find holiness and help Jesus to assemble material for the everlasting Kingdom, by and through everyday choices and tasks, was not in the picture. For the laity, achieving holiness in their daily toils was not so much optional. It was an impossible, if not an unintelligible, proposal. The *best* (if you will) the lay person could strive for was to perform his religious duties, obey the clergy, support the institutional Church, and avoid death in mortal sin so as to, eventually, get to heaven.

I

This impoverished way of thinking about sanctity should strike anyone familiar with the Gospels as very odd. There is indeed something special about the priesthood, as there is about other forms of consecrated religious life. But the thought that holiness and sanctity are limited to those in religious orders must sound mistaken to anyone familiar with the Gospels.

---

1   R. Shaw, *To Hunt, To Shoot, To Entertain* 10 (Ignatius 1993).

Jesus called *everyone* to follow him, to become his disciple. Jesus commanded *all* during the Sermon on the Mount to "be perfect, just as [our] Heavenly Father is perfect." *Everyone* is a brother and sister in the Lord. We are *all* called to be saints.

Jesus made it as clear as he possibly could that each and every one of humankind would be judged strictly on the merits, with the worrying addendum that to whom much is given much will be expected. Jesus also warned us "that [if anyone] shall scandalize one of these little ones that believe in me, it were better for him that a millstone should be hanged about his neck, and that he should be drowned in the depth of the sea" [Mt. 18:6]. I have never been able to track down the source for it, but knowledgeable friends allege that Saint Jerome, upon hearing that an acquaintance had been raised to the episcopacy, cautioned him not to think that just because you have become a bishop, that it makes you a Catholic.

Before the Second Council a few thinkers developed a theological understanding of lay action that would have, if more widely accepted, broken the fetters of clericalism and brought Catholics' understanding of the lay life closer in line with that of Jesus. Yves Congar notably contributed to the development of doctrine about the laity, as did Pius XII, in several speeches during the 1950s. More presciently, John Courtney Murray published two fine scholarly articles in *Theological Studies* in 1944 on the lay vocation. Murray also favorably reviewed in those pages *The Layman's Call*, a brilliant 1942 book by the Rev. William R. O'Connor. O'Connor emphasized that all members of Christ's body – lay as well as priestly and religious – are called by God to a particular life's work. Each and every Christian is graced by God with a vocation: "no one is without a definite call of some kind from the Lord" (18). Lay persons are called to engage in an apostolate that contributes to the building up of the Kingdom of God and to strive for the perfection appropriate to their state in life.

O'Connor outlined the doctrines of providence, nature, grace, and predestination with a view toward developing a doctrine of vocation as "a providential meeting of a suitably disposed nature with right opportunities for doing some good" (118). He deployed what he called the "analogy of sanctity" in asserting that personal holiness – conformity to God's will – is not a univocal quality the sole evaluative standards of which are the counsels of perfection to which only priestly and religious are called to aspire and live. Rather, what sanctity *is* shifts, without being purely equivocal, between various states in life and, more broadly, personal vocations. Each one of us is called to Christian perfection, to love God above all things and all other things for God's sake, and to carry out the role particular to his placement in the one mystical body of Christ. O'Connor maintained, however, the traditional view that vocations to the priesthood and religious life are objectively superior to alternatives, *simpliciter*.

No two vocations are univocally comparable; thus, it is mistaken to impose standards proper to one upon others. On this score O'Connor insightfully described the way in which eleven different lay states and professions (the soldier, the nurse, the artist, and so on) each in its own way serves the common good, builds up the Kingdom, and conduces to the salvation of the practitioner.

O'Connor's book anticipated the Second Vatican Council's teachings on the universal call to holiness, the apostolate of the laity, and personal vocation. Written two decades before the Council's opening session, one might think that *The Layman's Call* would have contributed to a flourishing conversation in American Catholic thought on the importance of the lay apostolate. Yet O'Connor's contribution to that discussion seems not to have been much noticed, let alone appreciated. John Courtney Murray was an exception; he favorably reviewed *The Layman's Call* in the influential journal *Theological Studies*. Murray praised the book for helping to "heal those shattered unities" between the natural and supernatural, spiritual and temporal characteristic (as he saw it) of those decades, and for its theological valuableness and genuine pastoral import.

O'Connor's book's footprint in Catholic theological literature of the period was minimal. It paled in comparison to the popularity of O'Connor's work on Aquinas' thought, particularly concerning nature and grace and the ultimate end of human action. Though O'Connor continued to study and write about the apostolate of the laity in the years leading up to Vatican II,[2] his work was not cited by the Council Fathers.

At the beginning of the Council the laity were vocational orphans; their call was derivative, secondary, and not specific to being a lay man or woman

---

2   *See, e.g.*, "Lay People in the Church" by Yves M. J. Congar, O. P., reviewed by William R. O'Connor in *The Thomist* 21.2 (1958), 229–234.

at all. If there is a counter-example during the twentieth century it would have to be Catholic Action. Pope Pius XII supplied the guiding definition of it in 1922, in *Ubi Arcano Dei Consilio:* the "participation of the laity in the apostolate of the Church hierarchy."

II

Even after Vatican II reinvigorated the notion that the Church is the whole People of God, Catholic thinking about vocation too often remained stuck in the premises of clericalism. One manifestation is ironic, if not comic: Vatican II is often thought to have *de-clericalized* the Church by opening up Church jobs to the laity, by letting lay persons do some things that only priests or sister used to do. As Pope Benedict pointed out in his 2010 address to the Scottish bishops, this is the tendency to "confuse lay apostolates with lay ministry," as if the laity are religiously active or holy or doing what Jesus wants them to do just to the extent that they get onto or near the altar. The altar is where the most important event in the history of the world is made present every day in Holy Mass. Parish involvement is a very good thing. But lay men and lay women can be holy – and can do precisely what Jesus wants them to do – without seeking a share of "ecclesiastical matters." Their path to holiness runs through Times Square, not through the sacristy at Saint Patrick's Cathedral.

Since Vatican II the Church has pretty much corrected old-school clericalism's *horizontal* limitation of "vocation" to a vowed few. Monsignor Talbot was on the losing side of history. His team was routed. We recognize now that *everyone* has a vocation. Perhaps more clearly now than at any time since the Council – and partly because the sexual abuse scandal revealed that many priests and a few bishops treated their callings as entitlements and as power – we are also vividly aware that the fundamental meaning of every vocation is *service*. We affirm that everyone is called to service, and through service, to holiness, sanctity, and everlasting life.

Bearing in mind that every vocation is service should make us all – especially those who have authority in the Church – humble. Bearing the true meaning and extent of vocation in mind should also make all of us – especially those in the pews – less prone to envy those who have more prominent callings. Bearing this in mind allows us to make greater sense of Saint Paul's comparison (in 1 *Corinthians* and in *Romans*) of the different charisms in the Church to the different members of the one Body. "There are different gifts but the same Spirit; there are different works but the same God who accomplishes all of them in everyone" [I Cor. 12:4].

Today, clergy and laity alike often refer to married life as a "vocation." Talk about laypersons' vocations is still limited to the big forks in the road of life: the choices to marry (or not) and of how to make one's living. This understanding of vocation lacks depth.

The good news since Vatican II is that the high tide of clericalism has finally gone out. The sad news is that the pool left behind is shallow: the *vertical* reach of today's universal call to holiness lags. There is a great deal more to the lay vocation than whether to marry or to remain single. In truth, Jesus is asking a lot more than that, of each and every one of us.

III

As long ago as 1965 the Council Fathers recognized that we live in a fractured culture, one in which the norms of success in business, in politics, in sports, in military life, and in our own patterns of consumption are poorly integrated with gospel values. In "The Constitution on the Church in the Modern World" (*Gaudium et spes*) the Fathers said that "[t]his split between the faith which many profess and their daily lives" is "to be counted among the more serious errors of our age." We should instead carry out our earthly activities so "as to integrate human, domestic, professional, scientific and technical enterprises with religious values, under whose supreme direction all things are ordered to the glory of God" [*GS* 43].

But *how* are we to "integrate" all our "enterprises" with religious values? With what sort of ligament are we to reconnect our faith to the secularized realities of work and citizenship of our day? After all, Catholics do not make the rules which govern the market and the public square. Those who do make the rules seem to be indifferent to what the faith requires of us. We recall that each of us is called to live a life of loving service. But servants do not flourish these days. We know that Jesus commands us "to be perfect as the Heavenly Father is perfect." But where is the comprehensive plan, according to which each of us could bring together what modern life has set asunder and so "perfect' ourselves?

All of us are more or less under the sway of the reigning ideology of individual authenticity of the Mystery Passage and the "identity" project of which it is a central part. It is of course true that each of us must decide for himself or herself how to live our lives; if each one of us is to be eternally responsible for our choices then they really must be *our* choices. We long to believe that each of us has a richer calling, a more comprehensive vocation, something not so *vertically* challenged as the "big-choices" shallows mentioned earlier in this chapter. We pray that the call to discipleship is to a life in full, and that it is somehow an opportunity to be a co-laborer in the vineyard. How might we reconcile all these discordant pulls: towards individuality but also to discipleship? Towards freedom but also towards truth? Towards service but also towards leadership? Towards authenticity but also towards following?

IV

What might we catch if we cast our nets out into the deep?

We shall find there that each one of us has a unique *personal vocation*. In the deep we shall find what Cardinal Newman talked about, in words quoted by Pope Benedict in 2010 during the during the Newman Beatification ceremonies. "God has created *me* to do him some definite service. He has committed some work to *me* which he has not committed to another. I have *my* mission" [Emphasis added]. "My mission" is a distinct and unrepeatable assignment. Pope John Paul II once described (in his book *Love and Responsibility*) it this way: "What is *my* vocation means in what direction should *my* personality develop, considering what *I* have in me, what *I* have to offer, and what others – other people and God – expect of *me*" [Emphasis mine]. In *Gaudium et spes* the Vatican Council Fathers taught that Jesus "assures us that. . . the way of love is open to all. . . [and that] this love is not something reserved for important matters, but must be exercised above all in the ordinary circumstances of daily life" [*GS* 38].

These are all unmistakable references to an *individualized* way of following Jesus, in season and out of season, in life's choices large and small. John Paul II wrote in 1992 that "each one of the faithful must be helped to embrace the gift entrusted to him or her as a completely unique person, and to hear the words which the Spirit of God personally addresses to him or her."

Make no mistake about it: recognizing one's personal vocation is not like getting a draft notice or a credit card solicitation. It is not a xeroxed newsletter. It is not a generic summons to do to your duty. It is not addressed "Dear Occupant." It is rather about discerning and then embracing a lifetime of loving and lasting tasks with *your* name on them. Open this sublime invitation and you will find your unique way of cooperating with Jesus. If you fall down on the job, what Jesus asks of you will never get done.

The single greatest contribution Christians can make today to our culture is to show that there is not only goodness and salvation in the way of the Lord, as unsurpassingly important as that Good News is. Today's world desperately needs to hear that there is equality and individuality and freedom in the way of the Lord. As Pope John Paul II wrote on the Fortieth World Day of Prayer for Vocations:

> How can one not read in the story of the "servant Jesus" the story of every vocation: the story that the Creator has planned for every human being, the story that inevitably passes through the call to serve and culminates in the discovery of the new name, designed by God for each individual? In these "names," people can grasp their own identity, directing themselves to that self-fulfillment which makes them free and happy.

V

The Council Fathers' development of doctrine about the *munus* of lay men and women is remarkable, even in light of the progressive vision of the laity that emerged in the mid-twentieth century. At that time, beginning with Pope Pius XI's *Quadrigesimo anno* (QO), the Church's pastors recognized that if faith were to effectively shape the temporal order, the laity would have to play a larger role in making it happen. But even these teachings envisioned the laity's newfound activism as an unprecedented participation in the *hierarchy*'s apostolate – as if the laity were deputies of the bishops, who alone had received the relevant charge from the Lord. The almost universal understanding within the American Church before World War II, for example, was that the laity acted *as Catholics* in the political sphere only at the direction of the bishops. American bishops commonly asserted, without a trace of irony or apology, that the laity were foot soldiers in armies they commanded. This vision unfortunately suggested that Catholic activity for the common good of political society was *either* at the bishops' direction, *or* simply "political" or "partisan"; that is, not meaningfully related to the Church's social teaching and thus a free range for lay activity.

This vision was not good for the bishops, for the laity, or for the common good of the United States.

The Council not only rediscovered, and revivified, the whole idea of personal vocation. The Fathers also described how the most distinctive call of the laity is to redeem the temporal order. *This* is the *apostolate* of the laity. The truth about the laity's calling emerged clearly, in authoritative form, only at the Second Vatican Council. Pope John Paul II wrote in in *Christifideles Laici* that the Council wrote "as never before on the nature, dignity, spirituality, mission, and responsibility of the lay faithful" (2).

The reasons for encouraging greater lay initiative were cogent. Altar and throne arrangements were almost extinct by the time of Council. Christendom as a cultural force was being rapidly spent. In some countries Catholic bishops could still pressure political leaders to do the right thing. But by 1960 this happened only in a few countries, and there less frequently, and then all-too-often because on other occasions the bishops collaborated (if only by their silences) with powerful people when they did bad things. Lingering examples of episcopal strong-arming were often subject to considerable backlash in less clubbable settings, as the conviction that political economy should be emancipated from clerical control and even religious influence spread among elites and common folks alike. International affairs, mass culture, popular education, the arts, and literature were all increasingly secularized. That laypersons would be the primary instruments whereby Gospel values could be insinuated into social and political life, through their example and by their choices, day in and day out, became an imperative (if you will) of modern life.

In *Apostolicam actuositatem* ("*AA*") the Council unequivocally declared that the laity receive their distinctive call to be "leaven" in the temporal order directly from Christ. It is not a share or participation in the hierarchy's apostolate. "The laity derive the right and duty to the apostolate from their union with Christ the head; incorporated into Christ's Mystical Body through Baptism and strengthened by the power of the Holy Spirit through Confirmation, they are assigned to the apostolate by the Lord himself" (3).

There are by now countless descriptions of this apostolate in the papal corpus. Lay men and women reside "in the midst of the world and [are] in charge of the most varied temporal tasks." "The *apostolate* in the social milieu, that is, the effort to infuse a Christian spirit into the mentality, customs, laws, and structures of the community in which one lives, is so much the duty and responsibility of the laity that it can never be performed properly by others. In this area the laity can exercise the *apostolate* of like toward like. It is here that they complement the testimony of life with the testimony of the word" (*AA* 13, emphasis added). The laity's field of activity "is the vast and complicated world of politics, society and economics, but also the world of culture, of the sciences and the arts, of international life, of the mass media"; their range of operations also extends to "other realities which are open to evangelization, such as human love, the family, the education of children and adolescents, professional work, suffering" (*Evangelii nuntiandi* 70).

The lay apostolate reverberates through the Council's descriptions of the bishops' role in temporal matters. That role is both overarching and subsidiary, both directive and supportive. "Pastors must clearly state the principles concerning the purpose of creation and the use of temporal things, and must offer the moral and spiritual aids by which the temporal order may be renewed in Christ by the laity" (*AA* 7). "The hierarchy should promote the *apostolate* of the laity, provide it with moral guidance and spiritual support, direct the conduct of the *apostolate* to the common good of the Church, and attend to the preservation of doctrine and order" (*AA* 24, emphasis added).

After the Council Pope Paul VI wrote in *Evangelii nuntiandi* that, while it is the "specific role of the pastors" to establish and develop the ecclesial community, the laity's "primary and immediate task" is "to put to use every Christian and evangelical possibility latent but already present and active in the affairs of the world" (*EN* 70). Pope John Paul II wrote about solving political problems in that "models that are real and truly effective can arise only within the framework of different historical situations, through the efforts of all those who responsibly confront concrete problems in all their social, economic, political and cultural aspects, as those interact with one another" (*CA* 43). He wrote in *Christifideles Laici* that the laity's distinctive mission required that they be "animated by a real participation in the life of the Church and enlightened by her social doctrine", as well as "supported by the nearness of the Christian community and their pastors" (42).

VI

This is probably the moment to observe that discerning one's personal vocation is not like asking: "What Would Jesus Do?" It is true that whenever we are confronted with a morally significant choice, we should be sure to keep the commandments – just as Jesus did. But keeping the commandments is about doing good and avoiding evil. We should all do *that*, though, quite apart from any concept of personal vocation. We should indeed strive to imitate Jesus's steadfast fidelity to His vocation. We should follow the Lord's example of faithfulness to the Father's will. But His vocation is not nearly the same as yours, or mine. His was, in fact, so structurally distinct from almost anyone else's that, the Commandments aside, one should be surprised if one were actually called to do as Jesus did.

Jesus did not have to make the choices we have to make. He was an itinerant preacher. Most of us are not. Jesus had no spouse, no children. Most of us marry and bear family responsibilities Jesus never had. Jesus never had to meet a payroll or get into graduate school. As far as the Gospels tell us, Jesus lived for years off the kindness of his friends. This is not a path most of us could walk. Or should try to walk.

Jesus' vocation was unique in a further sense. Jesus received his vocation from the Father. We receive ours from Jesus; at least, our personal vocation is to cooperate with Jesus in doing what the Father sent Jesus to do, namely, to build a Kingdom which He – Jesus – can turn over to the Father at the end of the age. It is not therefore a matter of "What Would Jesus Do?" It is rather about asking: "What Does Jesus Want Me to Do"?

Everybody is required to abide by the natural law of morality which Saint Paul told the Romans is written on even the Gentiles' hearts. Though following the commandments is not even a distinctively Christian responsibility, they nonetheless play a critical role in discerning our vocations. God is good and wants us to be good. God wills nothing bad for us and never asks us to do the impossible. The relevant "impossibility" is not only physical, like lifting a car. It is not only metaphysical, like (somehow) professing Catholic faith for one's faithless son or daughter. The impossibility is moral, too. So, if anyone should come to believe after agonizing discernment that he or she should marry the "soul-mate," who happens to be married to someone else or who happens to be of the same sex, one can be certain that one has discerned inadequately. God does not call anyone to commit a sin, and adultery is most surely sinful. Any woman who honestly believes that she is being called to the ordained priesthood is mistaken. Jesus willed that the priesthood be reserved to men, as the Church teaches in a manner which calls for the religious assent of every Catholic.

Personal vocation has to do with choosing from among *morally permissible* options. It is a matter of selecting from various good possibilities the one with your name on it. It would have been good for Peter and Andrew to continue laboring as ordinary fishermen. But Jesus needed a different service from them. Our young social worker rightly believed that she was cooperating with Jesus and building the Kingdom by her work with addicts. But her pregnancy changed her life and Jesus then had other plans for her.

VII

Anyone who judges that there *is* such a thing as personal vocation plainly has urgent reason to seek an answer to the following question: *how* does one come to know what one's personal vocation *is*? A lucky few come by that knowledge as a young Jewish woman named Mary or a Jewish persecutor of Christians named Saul did – by unmistakable and unequivocal divine communication. For some such fortunate souls the message might be as short and as sweet as it was for James and John, the sons of Zebedee. "Jesus said to them, 'Come after me. I will make you fishers of men.' They immediately abandoned their nets and became his followers" [Mark 1; see also Matt. 4].

Most of us will come to know what Jesus wants us to do more subtly, through a process of methodical *discernment*. Pope John Paul II pointed to what might be called the raw data of discernment: one's gifts, one's opportunities, one's training, and, most important, the needs of others within the circle within reach, so that you may act in a helpful way. There are several aids to proper discernment. These include prayer, frequent reception of the sacraments, good spiritual direction. Also, quiet. "We need to make space for silence," Pope Benedict XVI told a crowd of young people after he celebrated mass in Westminster Cathedral in September 2010, "because it is in silence that we find God, and in silence that we discover our true self." Then the Holy Father added, "[I]n discovering our true self, we discover the particular vocation which God has given us for the building up of his Church and the redemption of the world."

It is simple to see at the end of this book that the Mystery Passage and its "identity" corollary are counterfeits of personal vocation and the process of discernment which it entails. John Paul II rightly said that an "increasing number of Christians" have dulled their sensitivity to Christ's call "because they are subjectively attached to what pleases them, to what corresponds to their own experience, and to what does not impinge on their own habits." Even though one's personal vocation is individualized, one still has to put aside one's own agenda, one's dreams, one's "passions" in order to discern it. Dreams and passions are not necessarily bad; often they are productive of good. But personal vocation has to do with what Jesus wants us to do, not about what we want to do. One must always be open to surprises, as Peter and Andrew were. One should also come to expect the unexpected. Taking things *seriatim* if not fully in stride is a spiritual gift which tends to immunize us against presumption. For you cannot take it with you one cannot know when the end will come.

As we read in the Epistle of James [4:13-15]: "Come now, you who say, 'today or tomorrow we shall go to such and such a town, spend a year there, and come off with a profit.' You have no idea what kind of life will be yours tomorrow. You are a vapor that appears briefly and vanishes."

Appendix One

The Mystery Passage ("MP") undermines liberty and the rule of law. I shall make three points in support of these two judgments. The first is that the MP is all sail and no anchor. It mistakenly exalts the freedom with which one comes to hold certain beliefs over the truth, validity, and soundness of those beliefs. The second is that the MP's account of what public authority should do to promote freedom – basically, leave people alone – is innocent of real-world requirements for enjoying *effective* freedom in political society. Third, the MP leads to a kind of Hobbesian impasse in which the liberty to create and inhabit one's own moral universe darkens the door to the public square, making it impossible to perceive and accept law as the structure of free cooperation among persons for the common good. In the MP's world, legal constraint can scarcely be more than brute restraint.

First, the MP holds that *you* would be inauthentic, not really what you are, if your beliefs were formed under compulsion. In respect to some matters – notably including religion – this is largely true. Religion involves free assent to truths about the nature of reality and human destiny (among other matters), and it involves (in some way, shape or form) voluntary participation in such religious acts as worship within a community of believers. Some other good things, such as friendship and marriage, are good for people, in part according to the freedom with which they enter and maintain the relationship. To a significant extent, the freedom with which people seek the truth about such matters and the freedom with which they embrace the truth they discover, *do* contribute greatly to their flourishing.

But the MP goes further than this, much further. Literally, the MP holds that the voluntariness with which we come to hold our convictions about an apparently boundless array of questions is not only the earmark of liberty – it defines us as "persons." But this is mistaken. It is also potentially dangerous. The truth about the role of voluntariness in constituting each of us as the people we are is ordinarily denoted by terms such as "character" or "identity" or "personality." But "personhood" – one's status as a person or the fact that one is a person – ordinarily means what one possesses or is by virtue of one's existence as a human being with a rational nature. The confusion between personality (to a significant extent self-shaped by choices) and *personhood* is linked to the confusion between making one's own judgments about how things really are (defining one's own concept of existence) and the way things really are. It is important that persons make their own judgments about many things, but it is more important that they not come to think that they possess a God-like dominion over reality.

The MP identifies the ability to choose one's world reality with being a person. But this proposition implies that where the imagination and the will have gone dark, the person loses human dignity and descends to some sub-personal status. This implication may not make the MP a foe of freedom. But by so exalting freedom – understood as voluntarily defining one's universe – the MP is surely no protector of persons without imagination or will.

In fact, we do not prize voluntariness over correctness, as the MP suggests we do, or at least should do. No one really holds that so long as one freely chooses to believe the earth is young and flat like an Olympic athlete or old and round like most Supreme Court Justices, it does not matter which it is. Our schools and laws surely do not treat those beliefs as equivalent, and they strain to inculcate the one over the other.

If one's decisions or judgments about certain aspects of reality are false because, for example, they deny that some class of human beings has dignity and rights (the dignity and rights they truly have), then these beliefs do not contribute to one's own dignity. These beliefs do not deserve to be accepted by others (society) as autonomous, that is, entitling the person holding them to act upon them. Though the person holding them must adhere to them – otherwise he loses his integrity – he should be restrained; for he may lose his moral liberty to act on them by reason of the belief's falsity, of which he is by hypothesis unaware.

Consider the case of racism. Racism – the belief, for example, that black persons are indelibly inferior to white persons – is false. Holding such a racist belief is certain to lead the one holding it to treat black persons unjustly. These unjust acts should, at least presumptively, be legally prohibited. But racism also mutilates and diminishes the racist. The racist is not capable of entering genuine friendships, or into any other relationship grounded in equality, with a whole class of persons – all those thought to be part of the inferior race. And so Miss Daisy (Jessica Tandy) is the loser in her relationship with her driver Hoke (Morgan Freeman), at least up to the very end of the film. No matter how freely one comes to credit a racist conviction – and bear in mind that such beliefs come in assorted packages, as founded in science, sociology, history, religion, and morality – holding a racist belief is a tragedy all around. A decent society does what it can (within limits) to extirpate racism, to help make it the case that no one is a racist.

Second, the *Casey* plurality offered the MP as the organizing principle – the theretofore unstated rationale or genius – of a generation's work. Here is what immediately preceded the MP in the *Casey* opinion:

> Our law affords constitutional protection to personal decisions relating to marriage, procreation, contraception, family relationships, child rearing, and education. . . . These matters, involving the most intimate and personal choices a person may make in a lifetime, choices central to personal dignity and autonomy, are central to the liberty protected by the Fourteenth Amendment.

All one can safely say about freedom in the absence of law, however, is that persons are thereby left in, well, a condition bereft of law. Whether persons are more or less free without law is another question. I am not referring to the nasty and brutish life of people in the state of nature. I am rather referring to life in a hugely complex advanced society like our own. Individuals and groups in our society confront a huge framework of settled behavioral expectations and practices – a *culture* – which they are often powerless to resist, much less to commandeer and change. Persons and groups cannot call into existence all the opportunities, practices, and patterns which they wish to participate in and enjoy.

Third, the MP says that everyone has a valid (at least from the constitutional point of view) liberty interest in doing whatever they desire to do. Of course, no organized society could afford persons the liberty to do as they wish. What is obviously missing is an illumination of responsibility and limits, some common and reasoned account of the point, justification, or value of limits.

I say *illumination* of limits, and not the *presence* of them. For there is no question of there being limits, or of persons being held responsible for their choices and chosen actions. The sheer volume of law and enforced restraint in modern societies is not especially low. In fact, there is a necessary relationship between the utter volume of legal regulation and restraint upon what persons wish to do and the guiding principles of the regime managing the constraints. Put differently, it is not at all apparent that there would be less law in a society whose law was determined by the MP than there would be in a society whose law was determined by moral paternalism, by therapeutic criteria, or by the standard of forming good "citizens." And there might well be more.

Of course, the moral justification of legal constraint is, fundamentally, the *common good*. But what meaning can that term have in the MP's world of random morality and limitless mental horizons? The "common good" in the MP way of viewing things is just the liberty to inhabit a world of one's choosing. This leads, however, to a zero sum game, in which *A's* liberty to do X – say, to be free from being seduced – simply takes away from *B's* liberty to seduce. B has, or may well have, no *reason* to be chaste, or to respect the integrity of A's body, save fear of consequences.

This impasse is structurally similar to that engineered by Hobbes, who thought and taught that men had the most rights – and the largest liberty – in a state of nature, a hypothetical location bereft of legally enforced obligation. "[I]n such a condition, every man has a [r]ight to every thing; even to one another['s] body." But is this not also to say that no one has a duty to respect another's body? Is it not to say, then, that no one has a right to bodily integrity? Where law supervenes upon this understanding of rights and duties, legal constraints cannot be experienced as the recognition of pre-existing moral duties, such as the Golden Rule.

That is, in the world of the MP, legal constraints cannot be experienced as the reasonable requirements of free and fair cooperation among persons for the common good. *Or they are so experienced purely by accident, by random overlap between what the law stipulates and someone's moral universe*. Legal constraint in this way of understanding law and liberty has no internal guidance to avoid being understood, received, and experienced instead as brute restraint, shackles, fetters, and gross imposition, which by definition subtract one-for-one from genuine liberty.

Appendix Two

Doctors Paul McHugh, Paul Hruz, and Lawrence Mayer submitted a courageous argument to the United States Supreme Court in the case of
Gloucester County School Board v. G.G. In an *amicus* brief I filed for them
they (we) argued on medical and psychological grounds that "compelled
affirmation" policies, along with the pharmaceutical interventions (puberty
suppressants and cross-sex hormones) that they almost always include, constitute *abuse* of the "transgendered" child. Here are excerpts from the brief,
filed on January 10, 2017:

> "*Amici* do not in this Brief address the considerable distress that
> some children (a little girl, say) are likely to experience if they
> are exposed in a bathroom, shower, or locker room to someone
> who identifies as being her sex (female), but who is, according
> to all or most appearances, a member of the opposite sex (male).
> *Amici* instead focus on the children these policies are intended
> to help – those (like Respondent) who are "transgendered" in
> that they have an insistent, persistent and consistent identifi-
> cation as the opposite sex.... But no matter how disturbing this
> condition of *gender dysphoria* may be, nothing about it affects
> the objective reality that those suffering from it remain the male
> or female persons that they were at conception, at birth, and
> thereafter – any more than an anorexic's belief that she is over-
> weight changes the fact that she is, in reality, slender.... Policies
> and protocols that treat children who experience gender-atyp-
> ical thoughts or behavior as if they belong to the opposite sex,
> on the contrary, interfere with the natural progress of psycho-
> sexual development. Such treatments encourage a gender dys-
> phoric child like the [child in this case] to adhere to his or her

false belief that he or she is the opposite sex. These treatments would help the child to maintain his or her delusion but with less distress by, among other aspects, requiring others in the child's life to go along with the charade. This is essentially what the Fourth Circuit is requiring here. Importantly, there are no long-term, longitudinal, control studies that support the use of gender-affirming policies and treatments for gender dysphoria. [Citation omitted] The [lower court's] mandated gender-affirming therapy is therefore a novel experiment. In light of all the existing scientific evidence – some more of which we shall explore forthwith – it amounts to nothing more than quackery... The [lower court] has mandated an experimental "one-size-fits-all" policy of gender affirmance. Underlying that directive is the assumption that treating gender dysphoric children in accordance with their self-proclaimed gender identity rather than their biological sex is beneficial to them. But there is no scientific evidence to support that rosy presupposition; on the contrary, the evidence shows that affirming any child's mistaken belief that he or she is a prisoner of the wrong body is ultimately harmful to that child. We agree with the American College of Pediatricians' conclusion that conditioning children into believing that a lifetime of impersonating someone of the opposite sex, achievable only through chemical and surgical interventions, is a form of child abuse."